a pocketf

RHYME

Imagination for a new generation

2006 Poetry Competition for 7-11 year-olds

YoungWriters

Scotland Vol I

Edited by Angela Fairbrace

 Young**Writers**

First published in Great Britain in 2006 by:
Young Writers
Remus House
Coltsfoot Drive
Peterborough
PE2 9JX
Telephone: 01733 890066
Website: www.youngwriters.co.uk

SB ISBN 1 84602 434 X

Foreword

Young Writers was established in 1991 and has been passionately devoted to the promotion of reading and writing in children and young adults ever since. The quest continues today. Young Writers remains as committed to the nurturing of poetic and literary talent as ever.

This year's Young Writers competition has proven as vibrant and dynamic as ever and we are delighted to present a showcase of the best poetry from across the UK and in some cases overseas. Each poem has been selected from a wealth of *A Pocketful Of Rhyme* entries before ultimately being published in this, our fourteenth primary school poetry series.

Once again, we have been supremely impressed by the overall quality of the entries we have received. The imagination, energy and creativity which has gone into each young writer's entry made choosing the poems a challenging and often difficult but ultimately hugely rewarding task - the general high standard of the work submitted ensured this opportunity to bring their poetry to a larger appreciative audience.

We sincerely hope you are pleased with this final collection and that you will enjoy *A Pocketful Of Rhyme Scotland Vol I* for many years to come.

Contents

Neil Brown (11)	17
Rachael Sewell (11)	18
Rebecca Oliver (11)	18
Greg Sinclair (11)	19
Pamela Clark (11)	19
Kirsty Henderson (11)	20
James Tiley (11)	20
Gregor Massie (9)	21
Daniel Comrie (11)	21
Ryan Oliver (9)	22
Tom Horn (11)	22
Rebecca Amy Livingston (11)	23
Kerry McKiddie (11)	23
Elizabethmary Stewart (9)	24

Antonine Primary School, Bonnybridge

Charlie Smith (10)	24
Allan Farrell (10)	24
Euan McCreadie (10)	25
Demi Anderson (10)	25
Jordan Strang (10)	25
Beth Haddow (11)	26
Emma Aitken (10)	26
Chloe Peat (11)	27
Kim Kelly (10)	27
Darren Liddell (10)	28
Kyle Gordon (10)	28
Melissa Jane Campbell (11)	28
Liam McConkey (10)	29
Emma Brannan (10)	29
Robert Hamilton (10)	29
Rebecca Spicer (10)	29
Victoria Dunsmore (11)	30
Elliot McMenemy (11)	30
Sophie Whiteford (11)	30
Ewan Anderson (11)	31

Ardgour Primary School, Ardgour

Alexandra Clark (9)	31
Rebecca Mackellar (11)	32

Kyle Davidson (10)	32
Karen MacAskill (10)	33

Ashley Road Primary School, Aberdeen

Keith Adams (11)	33
Mohsin Khan (11)	34
Hugh Cruickshank (11)	34
Geraldine Cooper (11)	35
Jason Angus Ramsay Smith (11)	35
Claire Innes (11)	36
Gordon West (11)	36
Miya Marnoch (11)	37
Greg Alexander (11)	37
Charlie Watson (11)	38
Kate Angus (11)	38
Kalle Leopoldt (11)	39
Hannah Brooks (8)	39
Emma Alderson (7)	40
Campbell McKendrick (11)	40
Tom Perritt (11)	41
Michael Gordon (11)	41
Meg Lough (11)	42
Lewis Clark (11)	42
Thomas Rowbotham (8)	43
Holly Allan (8)	43
Finn Muller (11)	44
Susanna Ingold (11)	44
Alexandra Ross (11)	45
Finlay McRobert (8)	45
Rebecca Fennell (11)	46
Callum Michie (11)	46
Rebecca Bee (11)	47
Bethany Lamont (11)	48
Lewis Seaman (8)	49
Annie Metzger (8)	50

Auchinraith Primary School, Blantyre

Jennifer Welsh	51

Balgownie Primary School, Bridge of Don

Lee Hepburn (11)	52
Duncan McBain (11)	53
Kirstie Polush (11)	54
Andrew Ewen (11)	55
Nicole Anne McCall (11)	56
Lauren Davie (11)	57
Ryan Black (11)	58
Rebecca Louise Lawrie (11)	59
Rebecca Hendry (11)	60
Robert Fairhurst (12)	61
Alex Smith (11)	62
Laura Bain (11)	63
Fraser Benzie (11)	64
Kirsty Louise Deary (11)	65
Kieran Anderson (11)	66
Sean Hanratty (11)	67
Laura Crookston (11)	67
Mark Christie (11)	67
Keith Sutherland Alexander (11)	68
Scott Forrest (11)	69

Ballantrae Primary School, Ballantrae

Kerr Cowan (9)	69
Ross Drummond (9)	69
Georgia Dorrington (9)	70
Gemma Morrison (9)	70
Ruadhan Cowan (8)	70
Laura Shankland (8)	71
Jamie Patterson (8)	71
Kayleigh Taylor (8)	71
Louise Carle (9)	72
Douglas Robert Buchanan (8)	72
Christine Flynn (8)	72

Barr Primary School, Barr

Abigail McGradey (7)	73
Daniel Connon (9)	73
Catrina Scobie (8)	74
Katherine Sherry (8)	74

Jack Smith (7)	74
Heather Lorimer (7)	75
James White (7)	75
Joe Adams (8)	75
Joanne Milroy (8)	76
Joseph Connon (7)	76
Jamie Lorimer (8)	76

Barthol Chapel School, Inverurie

Rebecca Watt	77
Matthew Watt (9)	77
Ryan Sloan (10)	78
Nathan Kirk	78
Mary Williams (10)	79
Amanda Walker (11)	79
Charlotte Cooke (10)	80
Bobbie	80
Drew Cowie, Callum Keys & Kieran Booth (10)	81
Jamie Strathearn (10)	81
Emma Simpson (9)	82
Lee-Ann Donald (11)	82
Angus Bruce-Gardner (11)	83

Belmont Primary School, Stranraer

Seona Corbett (11)	83
Nicola Small (11)	84
Jasmine Dickson (11)	84
Jemma McNeillie (11)	85
Ross Shankly (11)	85
James Caldwell (11)	86
Kayleigh McWhirter (11)	86
Lewis Dunn (11)	87
Paige Castle (11)	87
Ashley Hughes (11)	88
Rachel McCormick (11)	88
Gina Louise Ellis (11)	89
Nicola Reay (11)	89
Charlene (11)	90
Lori Moore (11)	90
Emma Breadon (11)	91
John Dalrymple (11)	92

Scott Gibson (11)	93
Rebecca Hannah (11)	94
Laura Casey (11)	95
Louise Connor (11)	96

Bervie Primary School, Inverbervie

Amy Barbour (11)	96
Amy Shand (11)	97
Kirsty Archibald (11)	97
Rachel Criggie (11)	98
Michael Anderson (11)	98
Kyle Leslie (11)	99
Nathaneal Wilson (11)	99
Alex Scott (11)	99
Joanne Stirling (11)	100
Ryan Stewart (11)	100
Josh Filson (11)	100
Alexander Jones (11)	101
Krysta Stewart (11)	101
Blair Stephen (10)	101
Daniel Lovick (11)	102
Scott Dow (11)	102
Stuart Lownie (10)	102
Ailish Lyall (10)	103
Lesa Galloway (10)	103
Martyn Horner (10)	103
Paige Lamont (10)	104
Samantha Wood (10)	104
Corey Fowler (10)	105
Callum Clark (10)	105
Cameron Donaldson (11)	106
Kyle Casson (10)	106
Holly Donald (10)	107
Daniel Bland (10)	107
Calum Tait (10)	108

Brora Primary School, Brora

Andrew Floydd (11)	108
Liam Sutherland (11)	109
Jennifer Robertson (11)	109
Carl Anderson (11)	110

Heather Carter (11)   110
Andrew Sutherland (11)   111
Lauren Miller (11)   111
Sol Campbell (11)   112
Sophie Taylor (11)   112
Allen Martin (11)   113
Lois Colvin (11)   113
Euan Cameron (11)   114
Mark David Keith (11)   114
Connor Simmonds (11)   115
Jack McNee (11)   115
Samantha Clack (11)   116
Jodie Grant (11)   116
Ruth Liddell (11)   117
Stuart Campbell (11)   117
Bruce Sutherland (11)   118

Campie Primary School, Musselburgh
Jamie Clark (10)   118

Carolside Primary School, Clarkston
Euan Shedden (10)   118
Lewis MacLeod (8)   119
Lorna Beattie (10)   119
Amanda Carlin (10)   120
Rachel Hannah (10)   120
Clare MacLeod (8)   121
Amy Johnston (10)   121
Jemma Blanchflower (11)   122
Aniket Kumar (10)   122
Cara Sneddon (11)   123
Andrew Warnock (8)   123
Callum Tarvit (8)   124
Ross Landsburgh (11)   124
Jordan Black (8)   125
Fiona Clyde (8)   126
Laura Forbes (8)   127
Aimee McKinven (11)   128
Humza Ismail (11)   129
Craig O'Brien (11)   129
Cameron Reid (11)   130

Christopher Anderson (11)	130
Laura McAughtrie (11)	131
Ryan Bell (11)	131
Maaria Zabir (11)	132
Waqas Hussain (11)	132
Sarah Beattie (11)	133
Hazel Thompson (11)	133
Nathan Zochowski (10)	134
Ross Gunning (11)	134
Callum Sweeney (11)	135
Karen Barclay (11)	136
Aimee Kay (11)	137
Freyja Wilson (11)	138
Kirsten MacGregor (11)	139
Ross Brown (11)	139
Timothy Dunn (10)	140

Cathedral Primary School, Motherwell

Rachael Lamarra (11)	140
Chloe McAlpine (11)	141
Erin Eadie (11)	142
Claire Connelly (11)	143
Rachel McCann (11)	144
Shaun Nicholls (11)	145
Natalie Thomson (11)	145
Bobbie Paterson (11)	146
Jordan Lewis (11)	146
Mhairi Duncan (11)	147
Rebecca Fitzsimmons (11)	147
Colette Carr (10)	148
Amy Stark (11)	148
Aimee Flanagan (11)	149
Stefan Ward (11)	149
Shaun Donnelly (11)	150
Michael McCabe (11)	150
Sarah Lloyd (11)	151
Fiona Ross (11)	151
Nicole Leggate (11)	152
Lauren McShannon (11)	152
Katie Cunningham (11)	153

Cawburn Community Primary School, Pumpherston

Cleish Primary School, Cleish

Clerkhill Primary School, Peterhead

Colliston Primary School, Colliston

Crail Primary School, Crail

Scott Patterson (11)	168
Lisa Mowbray (10)	169
Sean Barnes (10)	169
Nicola Mayes (10)	170
Anthony Mitchell (10)	170
Ruth Dickson (10)	171
Megan Reilly (9)	171
Hazel Forgan (9)	172
Lauren Brown (9)	172
David Morales Miller (10)	172
Laura Wilson (10)	173
Claire Thomson (10)	173
Peter Rhodes (10)	174

Crathes Primary School, Crathes

Scott Bramley (9)	174
Nicole Galloway (9)	175
Hamish Leeson (8)	175
Rhayzl Park (8)	176

The Poems

Days Of The Week

Monday is the worst
I think it must be cursed
Tuesday isn't so bad
When it's Tuesday, I'm really glad
Wednesday isn't good or bad
But sometimes it makes me really mad
Thursday, well, it's OK
Because there's lots of games to play
Friday, not my best
Sometimes it's a pest
Saturday, *hooray*
Today I can lie in my bed all day
Sunday, a perfect day
The day you can say, 'Bye, I'm out for the day!'

Lauren Shand (9)

I Feel Uneasy

I'm walking my dog in the park,
I think there's someone behind me.
Something creeping up on me,
But when I turn around, there's nothing there.
Something rustles in the grass,
I think I'm being followed.
I turn around again, something dashes into a bush.
Green eyes stare at me,
I look at my watch, it's 8 o'clock.
I call for my dog,
I feel uneasy.
Out it bounds, the thing in the bush,
It was only my dog!

Cassandra Casson (10)

The Tiger

The tiger behind the bars of his cage growls
The tiger behind the bars of his cage snarls
The tiger behind the bars of his cage roars
Then he thinks . . .
It would be nice not to be behind bars all the time
Because they spoil my view
I wish I were wild, not to show
But if I were wild, hunters might shoot me
But if I were wild, food might poison me
But if I were wild, water might drown me
Then he stops thinking . . .
And . . .
The tiger behind the bars of his cage growls
The tiger behind the bars of his cage snarls
The tiger behind the bars of his cage roars.

Frankie Moran (11)

Captain Scarlet, The Mysterons And Me

A bit of a nightmare.

They look funny, they look weird
They are round, hanging in the air.

They have no face, no ears, no nose
They don't have eyes or a mouth, but they can talk.

They sound funny, they sound weird
With low voices they say, 'We are taking over London.'

They are green and horrible, horrible
I feel a tiny bit scared
In case they take over London
In case they take over me.

I'm in London.

London looks funny, London looks weird
All the buildings are round or arched, nothing square
In the middle, a tall, thin, sticking-up building
Different from the rest.

Captain Scarlet in the car
Puppet, superhero, looks like a real person
Has a gun
Shoots it
Pow! Bang! Crash! Pweerrrrr! Blast!
The round, horrible, green Mysterons are blown up
Split, gone.

They didn't take over London
They didn't take over me.

Callum Amos (6)
Achfary Primary School, Achfary

The Bomb

I was out in my back garden, lazing like a cat,
Happy as a hippo, until someone shouted, 'What is that?'
I looked up to the sky and saw a plane as black as night,
Scared as a spider because something wasn't right.
I sprinted like an athlete towards the nearest tree,
Climbed like a monkey, as quickly as can be.
The plane was like a lion, advancing on its prey
And then the bomb fell, right where my house lay.
I screamed like a siren and quickly clambered down,
As quiet as a mouse, I slowly looked around.
My house, it lay in ruins, as silent as the night,
I felt like a wounded soldier, unable to fight.

Jordan Orr (11)
Alvie Primary School, Kingussie

What Michel Does

He slurps like a huge, scary monster
He stomps like a great elephant
He crunches like a snapping crocodile
He looks like a truly wild scarecrow
He smells like a stinky, muddy pig
He roars like a magnificent lion
He punches like a big, fierce boxer
He plays like a fighting soldier.

Hannah Richardson (8)
Alvie Primary School, Kingussie

The Evacuee Norah

She danced like a butterfly in full flight
And sang like a small bird in a tree,
She cared like a queen for all the people
And was as brave as a knight going to fight,
She moved like a dancer on the stage
And sprinted like the wind when she wanted,
She sagged like a rag doll that nobody cared for
And she was as kind as a mother to her sister,
She was as poor as a beggar in the streets,
But as bright as the sun shining in the sky,
She was as funny as a clown in the circus
And she was as talented as a gymnast in a contest.

Jessica Convery (11)
Alvie Primary School, Kingussie

Soldier

As the cold, gentle wind blows,
When the heart of the field sings its praise,
As I fly like a hawk in the wind,
I feel as fearless as a stray lion.
As a dreamful echo sings,
I fly through a dream on fearless wings.
As we blow through the lifeless gates,
In the scriptures of the unknown scroll,
Life is a beat of an untold world.

Antonio Vastano (11)
Alvie Primary School, Kingussie

Billy Gale

She scuffles like a penguin down the stairs, pockets spilling oats,
She spies the door like a crow,
Prowls like a panther out of it,
She is as fit as a fiddle, skipping down the steps,
Shhhh Billy! Don't wake the house,
She darts like a hare to the pig pen, throws oats to the ground,
She struts like a peacock back to the house,
Tough as a tiger,
She eats like an elephant, gobbles her breakfast in one gulp,
Returns to her room, quiet as a mouse.

Siobhán Keegan (9)
Alvie Primary School, Kingussie

I Am

I am a little girl who loves animals
I hope that all animals are looked after
I try to look after all seven of my animals
I worry about all sorts of animals
I am a little girl who loves animals.

I see animals sad and happy
I wonder if I can help all these animals
I dream that all animals could be OK
I understand what animals need to live
I am a little girl who loves animals.

I want every animal to be loved
I feel as if I can't do enough for the animals
I pretend that all animals are OK
I say what I think about people who are cruel to animals
I am a little girl who loves animals.

Rhona Campbell (9)
Alyth Primary School, Alyth

I Am

I am just a girl who likes writing
I never understood poverty or war
I try to understand it, but I can't
I am just a girl who likes writing.

I think at night, will our world ever change?
I want to change, to change the world, but I can't
I hope it will change for the better
I am just a girl who likes writing.

I pretend that the world is a safe place
I know it isn't
I wonder how animals sleep at night
I am just a girl who likes writing.

I feel as if I am to blame for everything
I often think about the people in Africa
I hear sad things on the television
I am just a girl who likes writing.

Eryn Sinclair (9)
Alyth Primary School, Alyth

I Am

I understand the birds chirping on the wall
But the snake on the slide
I can't understand at all.
You see it slithers through the garden
It doesn't bother with me
I am just a boy that understands the birds.

I understand the birds chirping in the tree
But the eagle on the swings
I can't understand at all.
These huge, staring eyes are hypnotising me
With a flap of his wings, he is up in the air
But I am just a boy that understands the birds.

Sebastian Currie (9)
Alyth Primary School, Alyth

I Am

I am a football fanatic
I wish I were a cheetah so I was fast
I dreamt that I was the best footballer ever
I wonder what I will be
I feel as if I am king of the world
I imagine I'm flying through the air.

I am a football fanatic
I sometimes go to the Brazil games
I hear the crowd singing and screaming
I see footballs in the mirror
I play football anthems singing in my room
I try my hardest to get better.

I am a football fanatic
I even taught my pets to play football
I think I rule the world
I laugh when I see beginners.

Shaun Thomson (11)
Alyth Primary School, Alyth

I Am

I am just a girl who likes zebras
I cry for a better world
I say that everyone should agree and not fight
I am sad about the children who lose their parents
I am just a girl who likes zebras.

I am just a girl who likes zebras
I worry about families who are homeless
I feel as if the planet is falling to pieces
I see programmes on TV about people being shot
I am just a girl who likes zebras.

Rebecca Campbell (9)
Alyth Primary School, Alyth

Me And My Horse!

I am a girl
Who rides up and down
Jumps about, plays about
And runs all around.

I say to my horse, 'Come on, girl!' to speed her up
I cry when I fall off her
I dream about being a horse
I try to ride her every day
I wonder if she hears me
I touch her soft mane
I see her running around
I want to be the best
I hope I win shows
I pretend to have a horse-riding show
I feel as if I can speak to her
And she speaks back
I wonder if I will be the best.

I am just a girl who loves horses!

Holly Young (11)
Alyth Primary School, Alyth

I Am

I am a good boy who likes TV
I wonder what will happen in the future
I dream about it every night
I worry if there will be a World War III
I want to see what happens when I die
I am a good boy who likes TV.

I am a good boy who likes TV
I wish the Earth was a peaceful place
I see things, but I don't feel them
I try to say the world is fine
I pretend there is nothing wrong with me
I am a good boy who likes TV.

Connor Macdonald (9)
Alyth Primary School, Alyth

I Am

I am just a girl who likes horses
I wish for peace in the world
I hear the sound of badness
I cry about the people in pain
I dream about the things I see
I understand the meanings
I am just a girl who likes horses.

I am just a girl who likes horses
I say that war is evil
I feel as if I'm there in poverty
I am just a girl who likes horses
I wonder why people are so mean
I know that people destroy the Earth
I wonder why they do that.

Angela Coventry (9)
Alyth Primary School, Alyth

I Am

I am a girl who likes horses
I cry about hearing them die
I understand they have to die someday
I am a simple girl who likes horses.

I am a girl who likes horses
I dream a hopeful dream of life
I feel like I have killed him myself by long-lost, broken love
I am a simple girl who likes horses.

I am a girl who likes horses
I wonder how a little love could hurt so much
I pretend that nothing could have happened
I am a girl who likes horses.

Megan Young (9)
Alyth Primary School, Alyth

I Am

I am a little girl who cares
I wonder what life would be like if everything was perfect
I cry when I see my family unhappy.

I wish the world was a better place
I feel as if I am a cloud drifting off
I am a little girl who cares.

I feel like I want to stop war
I wish the world was a nice place
I am a little girl who cares.

I say what I want to say
I like my country
I like to play football
I am a little girl who cares.

Kirsty Chalmers (9)
Alyth Primary School, Alyth

I Am

I am a girl who likes tigers
I worry about the world at war
I hear the shouts and screams
I feel as if I am there
I hope the world will stop war
I wonder why war was made.

I am a girl who likes tigers
I want time to stop
I try to see what really happened
I wish the war would stop.

I am a girl who likes tigers
I dream about the global warnings
I think about war in Iraq
I am a girl who likes tigers.

Kimberley Stewart (9)
Alyth Primary School, Alyth

I Dream

I dream about Africa and other poor places
I want to help
I worry about the sea and land
I feel as if the world is cracking up.

I am scared to think about flooding
I want to help endangered animals
I hope people will look after the environment
I wonder, will the world ever be the same?

Duncan Pogson (9)
Alyth Primary School, Alyth

You Dunderheid!

We used tae hae a gled be he's noo deid
Cos ma pa shot him, he's a dunderheid!
He was a gid bird and was never bad,
He wasnae the type tae be very sad.
He said, 'We need to be a braw team!'
And I said, 'That's the way it would seem.'

Nathan Boland (11)
Alyth Primary School, Alyth

I Am

I think of cakes and sweets
I dream of piles of money
I want to go on holiday
I pretend that I can go to my own world
I hear cars revving up outside
I hope that it will be fun in the high school
I try to think of other people
I would like to stop fighting
That is what I think.

Calum Pogson (11)
Alyth Primary School, Alyth

I Am Who I Am

I am who I am
I am a boy who likes life, not death
I try to do good, not bad
I wonder what I will do
I don't know
I am who I am.

I feel as if I am being watched
I feel as if I am locked in a box
I feel like darkness is near and light is fading.

I see the world
I see what is happening
I will try to do good, not bad
I smell the fires of the world burning
I have seen kindness
I have seen anger
I am who I am.

I don't know about life or death
I can't change good or bad
I don't know what I will do
I don't know
But I do know one thing . . .
I am who I am.

Hamish Simpson (11)
Alyth Primary School, Alyth

Dogs

I am a boy who likes dogs
I wonder how people live with them
I hear that it is great fun to have one
I dream of one day getting a dog.

I try to get my mum to buy me one
I cry at night for something to cuddle
I say, 'Why can't I get a dog?'
I'm just a boy who likes dogs.

Callum Adamson (9)
Alyth Primary School, Alyth

I Am Me

I am me
I say what I feel
I cry when I'm sad
I want to grow old with the one I love
I worry what will happen next
I try to do my best in everything.

I dream of what it would be like to win the lottery
I touch soft fur
I pretend I am 21 and can drive a car
I see me on the television or on the stage, acting
I understand that everyone is beautiful
I hope you like this poem.

I think that the world should be at peace
I am me.

Ellie Forbes (11)
Alyth Primary School, Alyth

I Am

I am a boy who likes dragons
I wonder what would happen if the world was underwater
I hope the war will end in Iraq
I am a boy who likes dragons.

I try to understand why people die in war
I see things that do not happen, in my mind
I dream that I am rich
I am a boy who likes dragons.

I want things that I cannot have
I worry war will never end
I understand what is right and what is wrong
I am a boy who likes dragons.

Lewis Comrie (9)
Alyth Primary School, Alyth

I Am

I am a boy who likes games
I wonder who likes them as well
I understand what I am doing
I try hard at everything
I touch animals
I hear what someone is saying.

I want lots of games
I see waterfalls in my dreams
I know what I am going to do
I worry when someone is gone
I cry if one of my family gets lost
I pretend that I am someone else
I am a boy who likes monkeys
I am a boy who likes games.

Rhys Phillips (9)
Alyth Primary School, Alyth

I Am

I am a simple boy and I like football
I hear there are people getting killed
I see sad things each day
I dream that no one is unhappy.

I worry that people die every day
I try not to hear about bad things
I wonder what the world will be like in 2009
I cry when I hear that people die.

I pretend that no one is unhappy
I understand that the world loses people
Every day I dream that there is no pollution
I am just a simple boy and I like football.

Steven Bell (9)
Alyth Primary School, Alyth

I Wish

I wish I could win the lottery
I know I never will
I would love to go to the moon
I know I never will
I dream about working in a chocolate factory
I know I never will
I pretend I'll live forever
I know I never will.

I hope I get a job I enjoy
I can make it possible
I want to help a charity
I can make it possible.

I wonder what I'll be when I grow up.

Jason Campbell (11)
Alyth Primary School, Alyth

I Am

I am a girl who likes kittens
I wonder what lies ahead of me
I try to understand that people struggle
I dream that our lives will get much better.

I hope that we get along fine in school
I pretend to fly like a bird in the sky
I worry that the world is going to end
I try to work hard in everything I do.

I try to see happiness in my dreams
I cry when I get hurt badly
I am a girl who likes kittens.

Kaitlin McDonald (9)
Alyth Primary School, Alyth

The Future

I wish I was in the future
I hope one day to be in the future
I wish I was in the year 3000
I think about the robots.

I wonder about the future
I wonder about what it could be like
I want to know if the people in the future will remember the past
I worry about supplies and when they will run out
I wish I was in the future.

I hope there will be peace in the world
I hope we will have new ways of energy
I wish I was in the future.

Cormac McShannon (10)
Alyth Primary School, Alyth

I Am

I think wars should stop
I wonder what will happen to the world
I try to do well in school
I want to be a millionaire
I cry about my mum
I understand the world.

I dream I am a red squirrel
I pretend to be a samurai
I feel as if I am a raging volcano
I hope for peace in the world
I love animals
That's just me.

Neil Brown (11)
Alyth Primary School, Alyth

Bruno The Dug

I hae a wee dug that's clappit,
He is mad and he is glaikit,
If he gets the hump,
He might start to jump,
He cannot be an English dog,
Because he loves to lick the bog!

He often haes a collieshangie,
And aw body think that he's manky,
He chases craws
And opens his jaws,
He gees a leap and a bound,
Then he plummets tae the ground.

He thinks that he's aheid o' the game,
He thinks that he runs this hame,
Listen here and use yer lug!
Get to bed and get cosy and snug
You silly, auld dug!

Rachael Sewell (11)
Alyth Primary School, Alyth

I Am

I am a girl who loves making friends and smiling
I hope one day to see the sun shining and the moon glowing
I dream I can eat more chocolate than ever before
I smile as if I am the best girl in the world
I think of good, not bad
I understand that everyone is special, not just me
I cry when I am sad and lonely, but a smile is only a memory away
I am going to spread my wings and learn how to fly!

Rebecca Oliver (11)
Alyth Primary School, Alyth

Beth!

Ma dug is braw,
She's twa fit tae,
She howkit a hael
And found an auld pael,
Ma paw and maw love the lass,
We got her right afore Christmas,
So we cauld her Beth.

She'll licket anything from yer haund tae yer heid,
But if she's really bad, we'll pit her on a lead,
She harkit a the time from dawn till dine,
We a love ye tae death.

Ma paw feeds her on ene and a half scoops,
When yer bowl comes oot, yer going in loops,
But noo she hae puppies and they're great
We feed a the puppies on ene plate.

Greg Sinclair (11)
Alyth Primary School, Alyth

Me In My Head!

I dream I want to be a singer, but I am scared of singing in front of
people
I pretend I am a supermodel, but I am not
I think I will be a good fashion designer, but I am not sure
I wonder if I will make it through life or not
I worry about my friends, but they will be fine
I see the world go round and round cvcry day
I think people walk past us because they are scared to say hello
I want to be everyone's friend, but they don't want to be mine.

Pamela Clark (11)
Alyth Primary School, Alyth

The Field

The fields are fu' o' life
And growin' crops fae us tae eat.
Tractors gae thro' them a' day long,
Farmers see how green they are,
But also ful' o' bog,
What would we dae wi' oot them?
Well, I hope we ne'er find oot!

They love tae work and grow,
We'd hae na food wi' oot them,
Growing crops a' day lang,
See how tasty they a' are,
Available tae us a' year roond,
But there comes a price for awthin,
Awthin comes frae the fields.

Kirsty Henderson (11)
Alyth Primary School, Alyth

Ma Wee Cou

I hae a wee cou,
That goes mo, mo, mo,
He likes to chew,
A small but soggy shoe,
That is filled with a pile of smelly poo.

I took him to the milking shed,
To get milked by milking Fred,
But then he just fled,
To go to his bed,
He was nae fed,
Noo he's dead.

James Tiley (11)
Alyth Primary School, Alyth

I Am

I am a boy who likes monkeys
I worry about the war
I worry about people who are not as well off as us
I worry, I do
People who are not as well off as us
Are not seen fussing about what they eat or wear
You don't see them fussing, you really don't.

And the war, I wonder why it is on
So many deaths, so many tears, so many families lost
You can get two sets of clothes
And you can get two sets of food
But not two sets of people
At the end of the day, it's land or people
It should be peace, not war.

Gregor Massie (9)
Alyth Primary School, Alyth

Spike

Ma dug is awfae barkit
He's awfae sma' and clappit
Ma pa gets awfae crabbit
An' thinks the dug is glaikit
Ma dug is called Spike.

Ma dug digs in the gardun
We sometimes go tae the den
Ma dug scurries in the leaves
Chases rabbits round trees
Ma dug is called Spike.

Daniel Comrie (11)
Alyth Primary School, Alyth

I Am

I am a boy that likes the world
I am wondering what is happening to the world
I am the boy that is wondering what will happen to the world in 50 years
I am a boy who loves the world
I am a boy that wonders what people are doing now
I am a boy that likes the world
I am a boy that thinks about the world
I feel as if the world is going to live forever
I worry that the world won't live forever
I am a boy that likes the world.

Ryan Oliver (9)
Alyth Primary School, Alyth

Hornie

I wus takin' a stroll an' I tripped doon a well
An' at that moment I let oot a yell.

An' there I saw an unyirdlie sicht
'Twus the horned devil in a' his micht.

An' on his throne sat auld Hornie himsel'
An' next tae him a sma' feckless elf.

I tried tae escape so I climbed up the well
An' finally I wus back oot o' Hell.

An' a I did wus havier a' day,
Cos I didnae know what tae say.

Tom Horn (11)
Alyth Primary School, Alyth

I Am

I am,
I can hear birds singing,
I cry when I am alone,
I dream that one day I can be proud of who I am,
I worry what will happen next,
I want to be happy.

I am me,
I love my family,
I pretend to be famous,
I try to be a nice person,
I understand that it is hard for you to know what I am talking about,
But I am who I am and nobody can change that
No matter how hard they try.

Rebecca Amy Livingston (11)
Alyth Primary School, Alyth

Tipsy And Flash

Tipsy and Flash are ma wee guinea pigs,
Sometimes we even ca' them pinni gigs,
They dae need a afy lot o' care
An' they dae hae awfy long hair,
Soon they'll need a gaed hard groom,
Or they micht look like a broom.

Tipsy haes a black wee face,
With a tiny white strip doon it
An' Flash haes a brun wee face
An' an ear wi' ginger on it,
Oh, how bonnie they both are!

Kerry McKiddie (11)
Alyth Primary School, Alyth

I Am

I am a Scottish girl
I see Scottish animals
Like a rat and a cat
I feel as if I am wearing a hat
I do cry when sad things happen
I understand people can't always get what they want
I do wonder about some things
I am nine years old
I am just a Scottish girl.

Elizabethmary Stewart (9)
Alyth Primary School, Alyth

What Is . . . Fear?

Fear is like thorns wrapped around your body
Fear is like walking into a haunted mansion and screaming
Fear is like walking through thunder and getting struck
Fear is like walking thorns and getting scratched
Fear is like someone chapping at your bedroom window
Fear is like someone robbing your house.

Charlie Smith (10)
Antonine Primary School, Bonnybridge

Sadness

Sadness is like the Devil sitting on his fiery throne
It is like a big cloud of smoke floating in the sky
It sounds like Dracula laughing from the tallest tower
It is like trees wrapping round your legs and your stomach
It is like an owl hooting in a dead tree.

Allan Farrell (10)
Antonine Primary School, Bonnybridge

What Is . . . Hate?

Hate is like a rubbish tip filled with lots of rotted fruits and vegetables
It is like a thousand knives going *slice, slice, slice!*
Hate sounds like a big, horrible, haunted scream coming
                              from beyond the grave,
With rumbling thunder and lightning
It is a gruesome big cave filled with deadly creatures which could
                              kill you in seconds
Hate is the colour of *death!*

Euan McCreadie (10)
Antonine Primary School, Bonnybridge

What Is . . . Love?

Love is a red rose swaying in the summer breeze
Love is the sound of birds chirping in the old oak trees
Love is the smell of lavender hanging in the air
Love feels like a really soft, pink teddy bear
Love is a bright pink, glittery paint put on a wall with care.

Demi Anderson (10)
Antonine Primary School, Bonnybridge

What Is . . . Love?

Love smells like fresh perfume kissing your nose
Love feels like a little smooth stream
Love sounds like chirping birds in spring
Love reminds you of Valentine's Day that you can't wait for
Love looks like Niagara Falls on a hot summer's day.

Jordan Strang (10)
Antonine Primary School, Bonnybridge

Daydreams

Vroom, vroom goes the engine in ma wee daydream,
Ma tractor chugs along the road,
I turn into the field where ah plant ma tatties,
Up an' doon the raws plantin' tattie seeds,
Chug, chug goes ma wee Dexta.

Vroom, vroom, goes the engine in ma wee daydream,
A meet auld farmer Jock,
Ha'in problems wi his choke,
Ah gee it a wee kick then off ah go again,
Chug, chug goes ma wee Dexta.

Vroom, vroom goes the engine in ma wee daydream,
Gaun up the country lane,
Eatin' ma piece fae lunch,
Am gaun hame noo, cheerie bye!
Chug, chug goes ma wee Dexta.

Vroom, vroom, ahhhhhhh . . .
Ma maw says we've arrived,
Bit Maw a wis huvin the best daydream ever!

Beth Haddow (11)
Antonine Primary School, Bonnybridge

What Is . . . Fear?

Fear sounds like a ghost tiptoeing near you to give you a fright
Fear reminds me of my grandad coming down from Heaven
Fear smells like horrible cheese; hot and poisoned
Fear feels like a ghost's friend and him coming up to kill you
Fear looks like a vampire coming to get you.

Emma Aitken (10)
Antonine Primary School, Bonnybridge

Walking Alone In The Dark!

I'm walking home,
It's freezing cold,
I'm in the park
And it's very scary!

I see strange, black figures,
As big as a crow,
They look like monsters,
Coming to get me!

I hear whistling in the wind,
It's a spooky tune,
Like the theme from 'Jaws',
Hope there's not a shark!

Now I hear the trees chanting,
Like the dead have come back to life!
Then they start to dance around,
Like wooden, haunted hippies!

It's getting darker every minute
And now it's starting to snow,
So I run and run to get back home,
But I can't 'cause I'm lost!

Help!

Chloe Peat (11)
Antonine Primary School, Bonnybridge

What Is . . . Love?

Love is like birds cheeping on a hot summer's day
It is like freshly baked gingerbread men
It is like butterflies fluttering around on a bright summer's day
It is like when you first open your presents on Christmas Day
It is like a red rose blossoming in the park.

Kim Kelly (10)
Antonine Primary School, Bonnybridge

What Is . . . Terror?

Terror looks like a wolf howling at the big, bright moon
Terror reminds me of a haunted mansion with a gate made of spikes
Terror smells like an old man's breath and a mouth that has
never been brushed
Terror feels like an old rotten apple which is lying next to
the old man's bed.

Darren Liddell (10)
Antonine Primary School, Bonnybridge

What Is . . . Fear?

Fear smells like a pot of frogs frying in a cauldron
It reminds me of just me walking, lonely on the streets
Fear feels like a slithery, slimy, hissing snake slithering up your leg
It sounds like a couple of people trying to rob your house
Fear is a person kidnapping you from school.

Kyle Gordon (10)
Antonine Primary School, Bonnybridge

Daydreams

Ma maw thinks ah'm snoozing
But ah'm really fightin' lions
An' I'm swimmin' wi' dolphins
An' flyin' thro' the air!

Ma maw thinks ah'm cleanin'
But ah'm skydivin' aff a cliff
An' ah'm jumpin' oot a plane
An' ah'm screaming as I hear this
Melissa, are you cleaning?

Melissa Jane Campbell (11)
Antonine Primary School, Bonnybridge

Love

Love is like two people dancing lovingly in the sky underneath the stars
Love is like people hugging under the shining ball in the hall
Love is like two people's shoes tapping on the floor
Love is like the woman's fresh perfume touching your face
Love is like the man saying, 'Will you marry me?'

Liam McConkey (10)
Antonine Primary School, Bonnybridge

What Is . . . Hate?

Hate is like a charging bull heading directly towards you
Hate is like someone punching you and never stopping
Hate is a dog growling at you
Hate is like a factory polluting the air with smoke
Hate is like shouting towards my face.

Emma Brannan (10)
Antonine Primary School, Bonnybridge

What Is . . . Happiness?

Happiness smells like Mum's freshly baked cookies
It sounds like a happy child running in the park
It reminds me of my mum baking a Mars bar cake
It feels like a little girl starting to dance
It looks like my little brother starting to talk.

Robert Hamilton (10)
Antonine Primary School, Bonnybridge

What Is . . . Happiness?

Happiness smells of home-made bread
Happiness feels like warm water trying to get down your back
Happiness reminds me of dancing and singing in the shower
Happiness looks like my mum jumping around with joy.

Rebecca Spicer (10)
Antonine Primary School, Bonnybridge

A Barn Owl Kennings

An old chap
A swift sweeper
A mouse catcher
A high flyer
A seed muncher
A grass pecker
An elegant animal.

Victoria Dunsmore (11)
Antonine Primary School, Bonnybridge

A Mixture Of Emotions

A cup of anger
A thunder of happiness
A cry of sadness
A show of embarrassment
Is a mixture of feelings.

Elliot McMenemy (11)
Antonine Primary School, Bonnybridge

A View Of A Hen Kennings

A feathery bundle
A royal queen
An egg layer
A good runner
A bird splatter
A pellet pecker
An oatmeal scoffer
A sharp squawker.

Sophie Whiteford (11)
Antonine Primary School, Bonnybridge

Daydreams

While the teacher's teachin' blah de bell,
I faintae ma ane wee world,
Fae Edinbra Zoo
Tae Timbuktu
Ah travelled
Like the speed o' light
Ev'ryhing that moved
Wis eether extinct
Or just plain deed
A thought a saw an alien
An a couldnae believe ma eyes
When ah wake up ah'm sure ah'll get the belt!
Fir daydreaming in the middle of blah de bell!
But ah dinnae care 'cause ah'd rather get the belt
Than listen tae blabbety, blabbety, blah!

Ewan Anderson (11)
Antonine Primary School, Bonnybridge

Moods Of The Sea

Sometimes the sea sings,
As the breeze softly blows.
Sometimes, when stormy,
The wind gets wild,
With a deafening roar
And the sea crashes against the rocky shore.

Sometimes the sea sighs,
As the breeze gently flows.
Sometimes, when rough,
The wind shrieks out loud,
With ear-splitting sounds
And the waves angrily pound the sandy ground.

Alexandra Clark (9)
Ardgour Primary School, Ardgour

Sea Seasons

The sea prances
Over pebbles
Punching, prickling
In the springtime breeze

The sea slides
Across stones
Swishing and squashing
Under the bright summer sun

The sea swims
Over stingrays
Shattering and snarling
On damp autumn days

The sea speeds
Across seaweed
Starving and swirling
When the winter weather blows.

Rebecca Mackellar (11)
Ardgour Primary School, Ardgour

Dark And Dangerous

Dark and dangerous,
Is the ship upon the reef.
Seaweed wraps around the wreck,
To stop the moaning creak.

The wreck has died,
In the perilous sea.
Octopus and sharks and eels,
Find it the place to be.

Kyle Davidson (10)
Ardgour Primary School, Ardgour

The Sea

Gulls gliding up and down,
The sea, the sea,
Gulls looking for prey,
I saw them fly first today,
The sea.

Tossing pebbles into the water,
The sea, the sea,
Falling in the sea with a splash,
I heard them splash first,
The sea.

Spade and bucket in my hand,
The sea, the sea,
The waves retreat away from me,
I played with it first,
The sea.

Building castles in the sand,
The sea, the sea,
Then the tide floods in, washes them away,
I'll build them again another day,
The sea.

Karen MacAskill (10)
Ardgour Primary School, Ardgour

The Blitz

The houses are falling like dominoes,
People are crawling to avoid their foes,
Wardens are calling to all the heads and toes,
The siren is screaming, 'To the shelter!' where everyone goes,
The flames are shining like bars of gold.

Dead bodies are in sight of kids,
Searchlights are bright enough to see a lid,
Engines are a fright of untuned music of death
This is the Blitz and the Germans are here.

Keith Adams (11)
Ashley Road Primary School, Aberdeen

Fire Like A Tiger

The fire is like a tiger
Running around day by day
Fire is always burning like a tiger
Never quitting the hunt.

Fire is very colourful like a tiger's skin
Fire is breaking things like a tiger's teeth
Ripping through flesh
While fire burns, it's like a tiger
Eating its prey
And crackling its shaggy teeth.

Fire quickly strikes as a tiger
Picking up flames
Fire creeps as a tiger hunts prey
And the tiger is wandering across the Earth
Ready to kill.

Mohsin Khan (11)
Ashley Road Primary School, Aberdeen

The Eating Machine

A hungry giant storming through the town
Crunching up everything in sight.

A whirlwind raging down the road
Sucking up any car that ventures near.

A pie-eating champ thundering through the house
Ready to chomp up anything set out on the table.

A black hole in the deepest reaches of space
Swallowing up everything in its path.

All these things are rolled up into one
What is this horrible creature you ask?
Why, it's a Hoover!

Hugh Cruickshank (11)
Ashley Road Primary School, Aberdeen

Fire Lion

The fire is a ferocious lion,
Hungry and hazardous,
He runs calmly through dangers,
With his sharp teeth and crackling roar,
He races on wanting more and more,
Throwing up soil under his paws,
All creatures falling into his jaws,
Nobody really understands his cause,
Some are lucky enough to escape certain death.

And when the rain is pouring
And the relief is echoed through the forest,
The lion pounces on his prey,
Growing weaker and weaker every day
And still he overtakes and scatters to revive strength.

But in the colder days, in November,
When the frost on the trees is a sight to remember,
He no more presents his temper,
With his head withering to lie low,
He lies on the soft dirt,
No longer his breath a sign of hurt.

Geraldine Cooper (11)
Ashley Road Primary School, Aberdeen

Car

It is Death's eyes searching for something,
I watch it pick its prey, oh poor, poor prey,
It fires off like a flaming bullet from a gun,
The poor, helpless body lies calling for mercy and help,
The beast goes off to find more victims to kill
People run from it and scream as it recklessly kills.
Car.

Jason Angus Ramsay Smith (11)
Ashley Road Primary School, Aberdeen

Fire Tiger

Fire is a hungry tiger,
Hunting for its prey,
Waiting in the undergrowth,
Waiting there all day.

Fire is a hungry tiger,
Very sly and quick,
A bone between his mouth,
Like a tree with all its sticks.

Fire is a hungry tiger,
With his mighty claws,
With a dying antelope,
Burning in his paws.

Fire is a hungry tiger,
With a mighty roar,
He's still very hungry,
He is wanting more.

Fire is a hungry tiger,
Burning orange and black,
The firemen are coming,
To put the tiger back.

Claire Innes (11)
Ashley Road Primary School, Aberdeen

The Fire

Fire is a proud tiger,
He runs through the undergrowth,
Mighty and strong,
Then he pounces with burning aggression,
Roaring and roasting as he goes,
Scalding and slicing through his prey,
Licking his lips, smoke all around,
Biting and chewing, crackling as he goes,
Then tiring and sleeping, hot as ash,
Waiting and withering.

Gordon West (11)
Ashley Road Primary School, Aberdeen

The Icicle

The icicle is a big, shiny knife
That's slowly cutting in,
It is a silver sword
That's slicing through the wind,
The icicle is branches
On a bare winter tree,
It is the cold waves
Chopping through the sea.

The icicle is like a pin
Poking through the wall,
It's like a chandelier
Hanging in the hall,
There's an icicle on the roof
All alone and lost,
I think the freezing icicle
Was left by little Jack Frost.

Miya Marnoch (11)
Ashley Road Primary School, Aberdeen

The Fire

The fire is an angry lion,
Roaring proudly, destroying everything,
Sneaking through the house,
With nobody seeing it.

Its teeth are so jagged and sharp,
Its tongue burning, flickering its lips,
Coughing coming through loudly,
As the lion sprints towards its victim.

The fire's shaggy teeth crackling together,
Smoke flying everywhere,
As the angry lion burns brightly,
But then the firefighters' water
Puts the roaring lion to sleep.

Greg Alexander (11)
Ashley Road Primary School, Aberdeen

Fire

Fire is a killer lion,
Giant and deadly,
He starts off small
And grows until he is ready to kill.

The lion sprints about the room,
Looking for something to attack,
Eventually he finds a victim
And he pounces upon it,
He lets out a loud roar,
As he devours his prey.

He cannot be stopped,
As he ruins the houses,
With his razor-sharp teeth and claws.

After he has ruined the house,
The fire brigade arrive
And inject a water needle into the lion.

Charlie Watson (11)
Ashley Road Primary School, Aberdeen

The Fire Lion

The fire is a hungry lion,
With his fiery yellow coat,
His bloodstained teeth,
Dripping from his last catch.

He slyly creeps along the ground,
He stops, he waits,
He gets ready to pounce,
With his razor-sharp claws out.

He jumps, he hits,
His claws sink into the white flesh,
He stops,
He sneaks away with it dangling from his mouth.

Kate Angus (11)
Ashley Road Primary School, Aberdeen

The Blitz

I could hear the bangs and crashes
It was like hearing with dogs' ears.
Thud! Came another bomb
On top of a building
Then came the sharp sound
Of the air raid siren.

Seeing the horrible things happening
I just can't get it out of my head
People lay there, desperate for help
But you know you can't
The planes flying overhead
The massive fires.

The smell that night
I was in a forest fire, it was so strong
The smell of petrol filled the air.

I could feel the intense heat from the fire
I was going through an oven
I could feel the flack raining.

I could taste my fear and sweat
Which was pouring down my face
Dust was going straight into my face.

Kalle Leopoldt (11)
Ashley Road Primary School, Aberdeen

Moonshine

Moonshine, moonshine reflects on the blue sea
Moonshine, moonshine reflects on me
Moonshine, moonshine covers up the shining sun
Moonshine, moonshine bursts quickly like a gun.

Moonshine, moonshine shines in the dark
Moonshine, moonshine glows with a spark
Moonshine, moonshine shining so bright
Moonshine, moonshine light up the night.

Hannah Brooks (8)
Ashley Road Primary School, Aberdeen

A Leaf's Life

I am shut up in my bud
Dark and bored, but safe and cosy.
Suddenly, a stream of light bursts into my bud
And I find myself twisting and turning,
Finally I am a leaf.

There are children playing
And there are fairs and happiness,
I feel fresh and happy,
But day after day it gets colder and colder
Until one day, I find myself floating and dancing
As if I am on strings
Until I at last fall to the ground.

I look funny from down here,
I wait and wait but nothing happens,
Suddenly a gust of wind blows me down the street
I wait and wait again
Slowly rotting
I am now leaf mould to make new buds for spring.

Emma Alderson (7)
Ashley Road Primary School, Aberdeen

Fire

Fire is a bull,
Furious and red,
He thunders along the ground,
Charging through the forest,
Destroying everything in his path.

His temper is white hot,
With no limit,
No one can predict
What he'll do next.

His home is the forest,
He looks back
And sees what he's done.

Campbell McKendrick (11)
Ashley Road Primary School, Aberdeen

The Great White Rhino

Fire is a hungry rhino,
Glowing in the dark,
He charges around,
Destroying, destroying, destroying,
He runs around,
Claiming territory day by day,
He picks up speed,
Flying around,
Stealing lives.

He has a roasting temper,
Slaying wood and cloth,
Then suddenly, he stares you down,
With smoke streaming out of his nostrils,
Hunting you down.

He rampages around the region,
Getting dimmer and dimmer,
The great white rhino
Dying in the breeze,
He makes a great last call,
Fading whilst the night goes by.

Tom Perritt (11)
Ashley Road Primary School, Aberdeen

The Fire

Fire is a silky snake
Slithering across the ground
It snaps at its prey
With its long fierce jaw
It sneaks up on its prey
With a deadly hiss.

And when the fire gets angry
It jumps from room to room
Hissing all the way
Destroying anything in its path.

Michael Gordon (11)
Ashley Road Primary School, Aberdeen

The Fire Cheetah

The fire is a cheetah,
Racing through the undergrowth,
His yellow eyes flicker.

He spots his prey,
Stealth is all he needs,
Then he rushes to his feet,
Racing along, he pounces . . .

His teeth glow white,
As he bursts the skin,
Red blood gushes out.
He devours his prey,
With just the blood-sucked bones left.

The cheetah is full,
He needs to rest,
The fire is put out,
There is just a barren landscape to behold.

Meg Lough (11)
Ashley Road Primary School, Aberdeen

The Fire

A fire is a slithering snake
Thick and thin
He curls around poles
With his sleek and slippery skin
After a minute he spreads his body
And leaps into the next room
He rests his head on the armchair
And suddenly strikes at the filled-up cushion
The cushion is now hidden in his grasp
As a bleeper goes off
He calms and curls up
Despite what happens, despite
'Cause we don't know what goes on at night.

Lewis Clark (11)
Ashley Road Primary School, Aberdeen

Leaf Life

Here I am in my bud, snug, warm and safe.
There I am really bored. Then *pop!*

Now I am a beautiful leaf, grassy green but then it starts raining.
I feel really strong, staring round at the cars and umbrellas.

Then I start changing colour to red, to gold, then boring
                                        battered brown.
Then *snap!* My twig breaks, floating, floating down.
Then I land. I get stomped on by it seems like twenty thousand feet.

Then I rest.

When I wake up, I find myself in pitch-black.
Then I get dumped with loads of other leaves.
I get crushed down, now I am soil for other plants.

Thomas Rowbotham (8)
Ashley Road Primary School, Aberdeen

Leaf

Squashed, bored and tight like a sweet in the wrapper,
Safe, stable, secure, like a bird in its nest,
Very lonely, nobody to talk to,
I hear the wind howling like a wolf
Then one day I hear a *crack!*

I am free from the bud,
Stretching out like a snake uncoiling,
I am a grassy green leaf,
I hear birds making lovely sounds,
Children shouting, grown-ups talking.

I'm scanning the view over and over again,
Getting very bored, days get colder,
I change colour, I am red and brown then
Snap!
I fall, I am spiralling to the ground,
Waiting for my fate.

Holly Allan (8)
Ashley Road Primary School, Aberdeen

Fire

The fire is an angry tiger
Sneaking through the jungle
Silent, apart from the crack of sticks
He pops up when you least expect him
He leaps up and grabs hold
The jaws of death are here.

He leaves claw marks on the trees
Keeping them sharp for his next victim
He gallops on and on
Burning everything in his path
He sees his next victim
And begins to run faster
He stops
His red glow dies
The water has worked
He sinks down, down, down . . .

Finn Muller (11)
Ashley Road Primary School, Aberdeen

Jazz In The Dark

The sound of the soft notes,
Soothing the mind like a breeze
In the hot summer,
Its cool tone sends a strange shiver
Down one's spine - an electric shock,
Notes getting louder, but the same pace.

The dark room seems to be illuminated by the noise,
Like a candle in a dark house,
What is that sound?
The sound of life,
Why is it dark?
Half the world is dark to me,
What is this?
This strange but beautiful sound is . . .
Jazz in the dark.

Susanna Ingold (11)
Ashley Road Primary School, Aberdeen

What Is A Star?

A star is a bright bulb
That shines down on you.

It is a silver 5p coin
That lies on a black rug.

A star is sparkly glitter
That makes your artwork shimmer.

It is the twinkle in a person's eyes
When they feel happy and excited.

A star is a tiny white dot
That is on a dark piece of paper.

It is a precious jewel
So beautiful and special.

A star is an owl
Sleeping during the day and awake at night.

It is sparkly paint
Scattered over a painting.

A glimmer of hope
That you can always trust.

Alexandra Ross (11)
Ashley Road Primary School, Aberdeen

Wolves

In the night when you're asleep,
Out come the wolves as they creep,
From house to house they eat some beans
Not baked or runner . . . human beans!
They guzzle down when they're inside,
Then go back home with some pride.

Finlay McRobert (8)
Ashley Road Primary School, Aberdeen

The Fire Fox

Fire is a hungry fox,
Sneaky and sly,
His fiery red coat,
Stands out in the night sky.

He sneaks along the ground,
Looking for his prey,
When he hears a sound,
He quickly runs to chase.

He sprints through the forest,
At the speed of light,
He pounces on the mouse,
It squeaks with fright.

He stands on his hind legs,
Out come the claws,
He attacks the mouse,
With his powerful jaws!

Rebecca Fennell (11)
Ashley Road Primary School, Aberdeen

Fire

The fire is a lion,
Orange and red,
He pops up everywhere,
In the wild, wild earth.

And in the heat of the day,
He leaps,
And runs on a chase,
Leaving his deadly trail.

But in the cool evening,
He growls and purrs,
His flaming orange fur,
Extinguished in the dark.

Callum Michie (11)
Ashley Road Primary School, Aberdeen

Rhino Rampage

Fire is a rhinoceros,
Running from poachers,
Never stopping no matter what,
Never giving up no matter what happens,
He is angry, destroying anything in his path,
Everything and anything, no matter how precious.

He hides in every place possible,
Like a bad game of hide-and-seek,
He is scared and afraid,
Charging at top speed,
But the more he runs, the worse it gets.

But after a fierce and savage battle,
He loses his strength,
Getting slower and slower,
Getting weaker and weaker,
Cowering in a corner, he lies,
Tired, angry and afraid,
The spark in his eyes
Is the last glimmer of fire.

But he does have enough strength to say,
'Wait until next time.'
And slowly fades away.

Rebecca Bee (11)
Ashley Road Primary School, Aberdeen

The Blitz

In the dark, bombed streets,
All the laughter had gone.
Everyone was running,
Away from the bombs.

Flashes of light hit the sky,
Whilst the bombers flew by.
Dead bodies lying around,
Scattered like ants.

The rain is pouring down,
Like bullets from a gun.
The buildings are broken glass,
Falling to the ground.

Dust is flowing through my mouth,
Like crumbs from a leftover meal.
Smoke is stuck in the back of my throat,
Making me cough and choke.

I can smell the smoke,
Drifting through the air.
Whilst dust is rising from the houses,
Suffocating me.

I feel the buildings,
The jagged edges sticking out.
Rain is trickling down my face,
While I run to find a shelter.

Bethany Lamont (11)
Ashley Road Primary School, Aberdeen

Leaf

I am here . . . in my bud
I see, hear and feel nothing
I feel crushed up . . . but cosy
Why do I have to get crushed here in springtime?
This is so uninteresting!

It is summer! I am open!
I am a grassy green leaf!
I am dizzy but glad to get some air!
As I stretch, I can feel the fresh air
I can hear lots of happy children . . .
I have a great view!

Wait - it's autumn, I'm dry
Where's the rain when you want it?
I am a ruby-red leaf
Help!
I'm falling, falling to the ground
I feel like a discarded crisp packet . . .
Whoof!
I am lying on the ground
Oow! Ouch! Ooyah!
Children are treading on me!

It's winter
I'm leaf mould
I go in the tree
To make new buds in spring.

Lewis Seaman (8)
Ashley Road Primary School, Aberdeen

Life Of A Leaf

I am safe, secure, squashed in my bud
Waiting
Longing for air
I am crushed and cramped
Bored of just sitting here.

Suddenly, I feel myself breathing
I am out of my bud!
I am free!
I am admiring the view
I see children playing
The rain feels refreshing on my back
Now it is getting colder.

I feel the sensation of changing colour
I am falling, falling, twisting and turning
Finally I am on the ground
A child picks me up
I am pressed into a book
I am now in a scrapbook
Owned by a child
I am happy.

Annie Metzger (8)
Ashley Road Primary School, Aberdeen

Blantir Poem

Blantir, Blantir
Where did ye go?
Didnae matter wither
High or low

The ole boating pond
In Stonefield Park
Where we aw played
Tae after dark

Blantir calder waterfall
Wiz the best bit ae aw
But kno it's no safe at aw

Blantir speedway wit a buzz
The bikes sped round in clouds a dust
Hear the sound of foghorns burst
Aw it Blantir speedway

Auchintiber in days gone by
We aw played in grass dead high
Kno aw gone and houses and factories
Dawns the pale blue sky

Blantir, Blantir
Where did ye go?
Ye didnae go anywhere
Ye just started to grow.

Jennifer Welsh
Auchinraith Primary School, Blantyre

Christmas A-Z

A is for angel that shines like a star
B is for Bethlehem where the shepherds are
C is for candles that light up the room
D is for dance that we do round a broom
E is for elves that try to make lights
F is for fairies that glow in the night
G is for glitter that I put on my card
H is for holly that the berries guard
I is for inn that is full
J is for Jesus who was covered in wool
K is for kin that is the family I love
L is for lights that are shaped like a dove
M is for Mary who sat by the baby's side
N is for North Pole, Santa shows the elves how to hide
O is for oranges sitting fresh in my stocking
P is for pudding sitting, begging not to be eaten
Q is for Queen Elizabeth reading her speech
R is for robin singing on the beach
S is for snowmen we all make them like Jack Frost
T is for tree, are there some presents lost?
U is for umbrella which I put up on snowy days
V is for video that we always watch on Tuesdays
W is for winter, that's when it's cold
X is for Xmas, that is very old
Y is for Yuletide, it's the best time of all
Z is for zero degrees, wrap up warm and don't fall!

Lee Hepburn (11)
Balgownie Primary School, Bridge of Don

Christmas A-Z

A is for Advent calendar with a treat
B is for bells, the sound is sweet
C is for Christmas which is fun
D is for duck which is yum
E is for elves that help Santa fill up his sack
F is for frost which is spread by Jack
G is for gifts brought by Santa
H is for happy they got a bottle of Fanta
I is for icicle
J is for jumping for joy, they got a bicycle
K is for kin
L is for label on a present
M is for music sang by us
N is for Noel, the time we trust
O is for orange in our stocking
P is for pudding, sit down and start scoffing
Q is for Queen
R is for really big present the shape of a bean
S is for St Nick
T is for the holly, hurry up and pick it
U is for unwrapping presents
V is for videos about pheasants
W is for Wise Men who saw the star
X is for Xmas, you get a toy car
Y is for Yuletide, hoping we don't freeze
Z is for zero, zero degrees.

Duncan McBain (11)
Balgownie Primary School, Bridge of Don

Christmas A-Z

A is for angel on the tree
B is for Bethlehem where Jesus shall be
C is for children playing and having fun
D is for duck, yum, yum, yum
E is for elves rushing about
F is for family who never shout
G is for gifts that everyone brings
H is for happy, some people sing
I is for ice cream, nice and cold
J is for Jack Frost making trouble for the old
K is for king, wise, kind and mighty
L is for lights holding the tree tightly
M is for mistletoe where you kiss
N is for Noel which nobody will want to miss
O is for orange in the stocking
P is for pudding, so get scoffing
Q is for quarrelling, who will go first and who will go last
R is for Rudolph, if you're lucky you might see him go past
S is for snow, soft and white
T is for tree sparkling bright
U is for unwrapping, what a treat
V is for video, pass the popcorn so I can eat
W is for wine, white or red
X is for Xmas, make a wish before bed
Y is for Yuletide, you will enjoy or you will be mad
Z is for zero gifts, if you're bad.

Kirstie Polush (11)
Balgownie Primary School, Bridge of Don

Christmas A-Z

A is for actors that dance through the night
B is for baubles that shine very bright
C is for carols that children sing
D is for dove, what kind of peace will it bring
E is for eager to open your presents
F is for families who are very pleasant
G is for gifts which we hand all around
H is for home which is where we are bound
I is for icicles, above and below
J is for jingle bells that ring through the snow
K is for kind, which is what we all are at this time
L is for laughing while the bells chime
M is for merry Christmas which is what we all say
N is for New Year, which lasts only a day
O is for orange which you find in your stocking
P is for pies sit down and start scoffing
Q is for quay, let's go on a cruise
R is for restaurant, don't have too much booze
S is for star, which is what they all follow
T is for turkey, don't hurry to swallow
U is for unhappy, which none of us are
V is for very happy, hope those presents go far
W is for Wise Men who walked a long way
X is for Xmas, when Jesus lay
Y is for Yuletide log, my favourite cake
Z is for zero degrees, which froze the lake.

Andrew Ewen (11)
Balgownie Primary School, Bridge of Don

Christmas A-Z

A is for Advent, oh goodie, it's for me
B is for baubles that sit on the tree
C is for Christmas dinner, come dine with my mother
D is for dance, oh no, don't bother
E is for elves in the factory we hear
F is for frosty days are near
G is for gifts wrapped up tightly
H is for holly, we'll make it shine brightly
I is for ingredients for the food we eat
J is for jolly old Santa, we'll leave him a treat
K is for kin, we'll give them some Fanta
L is for letter, I'll write to Santa
M is for mistletoe to give someone a kiss
N is for North Pole, where it's totally bliss
O is for Oscar, we watch a movie with the family
P is for pudding when everyone gets along happily
Q is for quiet, when we sing a song
R is for robin that comes and sings along
S is for Santa coming along the Milky Way
T is for tree sitting still, in the way
U is for unwrapping all of my presents
V is for video when I watch it with my parents
W is for Wise Men following the star to where Jesus lays
X is for Xmas when we hear jingle, jingle on the sleighs
Y is for Yuletide which is Christmas when we freeze
Z is for zero degrees.

Nicole Anne McCall (11)
Balgownie Primary School, Bridge of Don

Christmas A-Z

A is for Advent calendar that you open every day
B is for bells that ring on Christmas Day
C is for Christmas that people celebrate
D is for dance that people do at Christmas
E is for Eve, the day before Christmas Day
F is for fairy that sits up on your tree
G is for gifts that you give on Christmas Day
H is for happy when people love each other
I is for ice that comes every Christmas
J is for jingle bells when Santa comes
K is for kids when they play
L is for letter which we give to Santa
M is for Mary, who sat beside Jesus
N is for North Pole where Santa makes his toys
O is for Oscar, that good movies are given
P is for pudding, that you have at Christmas
R is for Rudolph who helps Santa at night
S is for snow that children love
T is for turkey that people love at Christmas
U is for unwrapping presents, what you do on Christmas Day
V is for videos, we watch them at Christmas
W is for wine that people drink
X is for Xmas pudding
Y is for Yuletide for Christmas
Z is for zero degrees.

Lauren Davie (11)
Balgownie Primary School, Bridge of Don

Christmas A-Z

A is for angel, so high in the tree
B is for Bethlehem, where Jesus was born
C is for church where everyone goes
D is for decorations which the tree is decorated in
E is for Eve the day before Noel
F is for feast, when everyone comes to eat
G is for gifts, the ones Santa gives you
H is for holly that jabs you when you touch it
I is for ice cream which goes well with jelly
J is for Jack who brings the frost
K is for kings who gave Jesus the presents
L is for love under the mistletoe
M is for music for children to dance
N is for Noel the day of laughter
O is for Oscar on Christmas Day
P is for presents you unwrap on the day
Q is for Queen, who does the speech on Christmas Day
R is for robin who bobs up and down at Christmas
S is for shepherds who were in the stable when Jesus was born
T is for turkey on the Christmas menu
U is for unwrapping the presents on the day
V is for videos you watch on Christmas Eve
W is for white snow which we would love at Christmas
X is for Xmas the same as Christmas
Y is for Yuletide dance you're in for a treat
Z is for zero, zero degrees on Christmas Day.

Ryan Black (11)
Balgownie Primary School, Bridge of Don

Christmas A-Z

A is for an angel that sits on your tree
B is for Bethlehem, let's jump with glee
C is for carols that children sing
D is for duckling that your mum brings in
E is for elves that bring Santa's tea
F is for fairies that come to eat
G is for glitter that glows in the night
H is for hat, jolly and bright
I is for ice on a winter's night
J is for Jack Frost who makes it right
K is for kin to make everyone feel cherished
L is for letter that we write every year
M is for mistletoe, give me a kiss
N is for Noel that we all sing
O is for orange that we get in our stocking
P is for pudding, let's start scoffing
Q is for quiet, let's start singing
R is for robin, he's singing too
S is for snowmen, let's build them up high
T is for tinsel twinkling like stars high up in the sky at night
U is for unwrapping presents, hearing them ripping and crunching
V is for videos, hearing them buzzing and squeaking
W is for white snow, let's jump up high
X is for Xmas let's get ready
Y is for Yuletide log, let's eat
Z is for zero degrees.

Rebecca Louise Lawrie (11)
Balgownie Primary School, Bridge of Don

Christmas A-Z

A is for angels so high in the trees
B is for bows hanging on angels' knees
C is for children playing so nice
D is for dads paying the price
E is for events on Christmas night
F is for frost that is snow-white
G is for glitter so nice and sparkly
H is for Hogmanay, hip hip hooray
I is for icicles, so sweet
J is for Jack Frost and big blue bicycles
K is for kin, your family and a friend
L is for letters you have written to pretend
M is for music you can hear so near
N is for noise, do not fear
O is for Oscar, films on Christmas Day
P is for poinsettia, my sister had to pay
Q is for Queen's speech, near to her home
R is for robin sitting on the wrapping foam
S is for star that shows where to go
T is for tinsel that you can wear to glow
U is for unwrapping gifts from nowhere
V is for vase you get every year
W is for wine you take to the table
X is for Xmas, lit up with a cable
Y is for Yuletide dance, you're in for a treat
Z is for zero pressies, don't cheat.

Rebecca Hendry (11)
Balgownie Primary School, Bridge of Don

Christmas A-Z

A is for Advent, work up to Christmas
B is for bells that ring while you're motionless
C is for children with expectations high
D is for decorating that people do after pie
E is for eat, that we do till we're stuffed
F is for friendly fat man who comes down the chimney
G is for gifts piled under the tree
H is for happiness that is the same as glee
I is for ingredients we use to make cake
J is for Jesus teaching down by the lake
K is for kings who gave Jesus the gifts
L is for lights that shine so bright in the mist
M is for mistletoe hanging above the door
N is for Noel another name for the day you don't have to do a chore
O is for open, this is what you do to your Advent calendar
P is for pudding, which does not exactly smell of lavender
Q is for quiet, what every Christmas should be
R is for robins who bob up and down with glee
S is for shepherds who hear the angels sing
T is for turkey which can be sliced after we hear the church bells ring
U is for unwrapping the bit we love the most
V is for video, the thing to do if you're the host
W is for Wise Men who came from far and wide
X is for Xmas which is celebrated worldwide
Y is for yew trees at their prettiest time
Z is for zero the best temperature or below, because it rhymes!

Robert Fairhurst (12)
Balgownie Primary School, Bridge of Don

Christmas A-Z

A is for angel that sits on my tree
B is for bells that ring out for me
C is for Christmas that all is for me
D is for decorations that lay on our tree
E is for elves that make the presents
F is for food that is normally pheasant
G is for gathering, the whole family and me
H is for holly and berries that we can see
I is for ingredients for my grandma's Christmas cake
J is for juice that she also loves to make
K is for kindness that we do give
L is for love, letter and love
M is for mistletoe that hangs on the door frame
N is for Noel that also has fame
O is for oranges that sit in my stocking
P is for pudding, sit down and start scoffing
Q is for Queen, making her speech
R is for Rudolph stamping his feet
S is for singing, oh singing, isn't it fun?
T is for tidying the living room for another Christmas bun
U is for unwrapping all the presents
V is for vases full of holly and berries
W is for watching the snow falling on the ground
X is for Xmas, it's all around
Y is for yodelling and cowboy toys
Z is for zero presents for you and there will be no noise.

Alex Smith (11)
Balgownie Primary School, Bridge of Don

Christmas A-Z

A is for Advent that you open in the day
B is for bells that ring the night away
C is for candle that will light your way
D is for dinner to make your day
E is for eating all of your chocolate coins
F is for fairies that bring you joy
G is for gifts, I wonder what toys
H is for happy girls and boys
I is for icy, Jack Frost must've come
J is for jingle bells, Santa must be here
K is for kids, some drink root beer
L is for love, it's all around
M is for music, much too loud
N is for North Pole where Santa lives
O is for orange that's what my mum gives
P is for presents that we open
Q is for quarrelling, my mum won't keep coping
R is for robin with a bright red chest
S is for snow down in the west
T is for tinsel shining bright
U is for unwrapping, it's alright
V is for video about a fight
W is for Wise Men walking about all night
X is for xylophones that the little ones get
Y is for yummy food for my pets
Z is for zero degrees on Christmas Day.

Laura Bain (11)
Balgownie Primary School, Bridge of Don

Christmas A-Z

A is for angels that fly in the sky
B is for bells which ring all the time
C is for candles which glow in the night
D is for dancing which you do all night
E is for eating which you do on Xmas Day
F is for feast which you eat on that day
G is for gifts that you give all around
H is for happiness which goes all around
I is for ivy which dies in winter
J is for jolly which you are all the time
K is for kindness that you share
L is for love which you give all around
M is for music which you turn up so loud
N is for night when you hear no sound
O is for orange which I find in my stocking
P is for pudding which I sit down and start gobbling
Q is for quiet when we say our prayers
R is for reindeer, when will we see one in the air?
S is for star, see it twinkling in the sky
T is for tinsel which you see everywhere
U is for unwrapping all your presents on Xmas Day
V is for videos which you watch on the day
W is for wrapping the present for Christmas Day
X is for Xmas when you unwrap your presents on that day
Y is for Yuletide and seeing all the tinsel and light
Z is for zero presents if you are not right.

Fraser Benzie (11)
Balgownie Primary School, Bridge of Don

Christmas A-Z

A is for angel who lives in Heaven
B is for Bethlehem where Jesus was born
C is for Christmas, it comes every year
D is for donkeys, who take Mary to Bethlehem
E is for elves who make the presents
F is for fairy on top of the tree
G is for great joy
H is for happy like you and me
 I is for ice that you put in your drink
J is for Jesus that was born on Christmas Day
K is for kings who gave Jesus the three presents
L is for light and glitter
M is for Mary, who sat at her baby's side
N is for Noel, it's a French name
O is for orange that you find in your stocking
P is for pie, pie I love the most
Q is for Queen, who makes a speech
R is for reindeer that drive the sleigh
S is for Santa who delivers the presents
T is for tree that you put decorations on
U is for unwrapping your Christmas presents
V is for video that you watch on Christmas Day
W is for white snow falling in the snowy sky
X is for Xmas just like Christmas
Y is for Yuletide log burning in the fire
Z is for zero degrees, the temperature on Christmas Day.

Kirsty Louise Deary (11)
Balgownie Primary School, Bridge of Don

Christmas A-Z

A is for appetite that you have on New Year
B is for bells that make you want to cheer
C is for celebrating that Christmas has come
D is for decorations I make with my mum
E is for elves that help Santa all day long
F is for family and friends that sing a song
G is for gifts that you open on Christmas Day
H is for happy Santa who rides in his sleigh
I is for icy paths that we all slip on
J is for 'Jack Frost', that film never makes me yawn
K is for your kin that spends time with you
L is for letter you send to you know who
M is for music, fun and laughter
N is for night that gets even darker
O is for orange in your stocking
P is for pudding, sit down and start scoffing
Q is for quench, so start drinking
R is for robin, watch out for him winking
S is for Santa who gives children toys
T is for toys we give to girls and boys
U is for unwrapping gifts on Christmas Day
V is for very merry Christmas that you love your own way
W is for winter wonderland
X is for Xmas when the snow is up to your hand
Y is for your presents, big and small
Z is for zero degrees, the icy paths make you fall.

Kieran Anderson (11)
Balgownie Primary School, Bridge of Don

Prayer For 2006

May the world be safe for 2006
And bring peace to my family.
Let me be safe this year
Let me have a fun year.
Let everyone be safe
Give me laughter in my life.
I hope for the best in Glasgow
Let me have a successful year.

Sean Hanratty (11)
Balgownie Primary School, Bridge of Don

Prayer For 2006

May God stop all wars
And give peace to all mankind.

May the bullet stay in the gun
And the gun be destroyed.

May I enjoy going up to the Academy
And like all my teachers.

May my family be healthy
And happy.

Laura Crookston (11)
Balgownie Primary School, Bridge of Don

Prayer For 2006

May the road be free, open for prayers
Make the prayers fly to Heaven
Let everyone be good and helpful
Stop all the wars in Iraq
Make it all love in the world
Remember the holes in the ground
By the sweet dream of the sky
I wish to make new friends.

Mark Christie (11)
Balgownie Primary School, Bridge of Don

Christmas A-Z

A is for antlers beside the sherry
B is for bells, aren't they so merry
C is for children playing in the snow
D is for duck, no place to go
E is for Eve, the day before Christmas
F is for frosty, no one will miss this
G is for gifts the children so happy
H is for holly, oh so spiky
I is for igloo so frosty and cold
J is for Jack Frost, is he gold?
K is for kindness, don't eat the feast
L is for lantern the sign of peace
M is for mistletoe, give me a kiss
N is for Noel that no one will miss
O is for orange all so bright
P is for pudding having some tonight
Q is for queen a crown so shiny
R is for robin oh so bobby
S is for snow just like candyfloss
T is for tantrum, I am the boss
U is for unwrapping all that paper
V is for violin just like a scraper
Y is for Yuletide time for tea
Z is for zero, zero degrees.

Keith Sutherland Alexander (11)
Balgownie Primary School, Bridge of Don

Prayer For 2006

May we have peace on Earth
May war come to an end and never start again
May we have a safe year
May you spread happiness all around our world
May you make people feel better from diseases all over the world
May you save people that are at war
Please stop the chaos all over the world
Please forgive us for our sins.

Scott Forrest (11)
Balgownie Primary School, Bridge of Don

Sadness

Sadness is blue like the cloudy sky
It smells like a bluebell in the green wood
It looks like a blue ocean
It tastes like a big sour lemon
It sounds like a drum in my head
It feels like a sour lime rubbed on a cut
It reminds me of a big fat punch.

Kerr Cowan (9)
Ballantrae Primary School, Ballantrae

Love

Love is pink like a balloon
It feels like a big fluffy pillow
It reminds me of girls
It smells like perfume
It tastes like cake
It sounds like a little bird
It looks like a heart.

Ross Drummond (9)
Ballantrae Primary School, Ballantrae

Love

Love is as red as a volcano's lava
It tastes like freshly picked strawberries
It looks like a rose
It reminds me of boys
It smells like sweet perfume
It sounds like your heart beating
It feels like a rose petal.

Georgia Dorrington (9)
Ballantrae Primary School, Ballantrae

Sadness

Sadness is black like the night
It tastes like dirt
It feels like anger
It smells like the sea
It looks like hot flames
It sounds like a book crashing
It reminds me of sour lemons.

Gemma Morrison (9)
Ballantrae Primary School, Ballantrae

Fear

Fear is black like a dark night
It looks like an angry spot
It sounds like a man dying
It feels like something is creeping up behind you
It smells like a dead fish
It reminds me of a monster
It tastes like blood.

Ruadhan Cowan (8)
Ballantrae Primary School, Ballantrae

Fear

Fear is black like thunder
It feels like a ghost has crept up on me
It reminds me of the dark sky
It looks like a giant zombie
It sounds like shouting and screaming
It smells like blood
It tastes like gone-off milk.

Laura Shankland (8)
Ballantrae Primary School, Ballantrae

Happiness

Happiness is yellow like the sun
It tastes like gooey sweets
It reminds me of good memories
It looks like the sun
It sounds like a duck
It feels like slime
It smells like smoke.

Jamie Patterson (8)
Ballantrae Primary School, Ballantrae

Happiness

Happiness is yellow like the sun
It sounds like baby birds calling for their mum
It looks like a fantasy world
It reminds me of summer memories
It tastes like cold ice cream
It smells like flowers
It feels like soft pillows.

Kayleigh Taylor (8)
Ballantrae Primary School, Ballantrae

Sadness

Sadness is grey like my pencil
It feels like a weight hanging over you
It tastes like a plain avocado
It sounds like rain on a horrible day
It looks like a rain cloud about to burst
It reminds me of a miserable day
It smells like a cardboard box.

Louise Carle (9)
Ballantrae Primary School, Ballantrae

Happiness

Happiness is pink like roses
It tastes like a juicy apple
It sounds like people laughing
It feels like people having fun
It reminds me of when I was playing
It looks like people smiling.

Douglas Robert Buchanan (8)
Ballantrae Primary School, Ballantrae

Fear

Fear is black like the sole on a black shoe
It reminds me of the darkness of a dark room
It looks like a ghost
It sounds scary
It tastes watery
It feels like sharp knives
It smells like smoke.

Christine Flynn (8)
Ballantrae Primary School, Ballantrae

What Can You Hear?

I can hear
The tweet of a baby chick
It's noisy
The crackling cold ice cube
Melting in a glass.

I can hear
The chinking of coins in my pocket
The crunchy leaves in the garden
Under my feet.

Abigail McGradey (7)
Barr Primary School, Barr

My Gran

My gran is as soft as a puppy,
Her hair is like silk,
Her eyes are like golden rings,
Her face is like soft leather,
When she walks she is quite slow,
When she sits she is like a baby sitting down,
When she laughs she is like a child,
When she sleeps she is like a teddy,
The best thing about my gran
Is that she makes up silly rhymes.

Daniel Connon (9)
Barr Primary School, Barr

Love

Love is red,
Love is happy,
Love makes me think of my family,
Love is also pink,
Love makes me think of hearts,
Love makes me think of bright colours in the summer,
Love is the thing that makes me happy.

Catrina Scobie (8)
Barr Primary School, Barr

The Tiger

Creeping through the jungle,
Where no one can see,
The big orange and black tiger
Is looking for tea,
Catching lots of animals, gobbling them up,
I hope his next meal is not me!

Katherine Sherry (8)
Barr Primary School, Barr

My Future

In the future
I'm going to be a millionaire player,
Then a billionaire player
And I'll score lots of goals,
I'll live in a big house,
With everything I need
And drive a Mazda RX-7,
Driving here and there
And fans cheering everywhere.

Jack Smith (7)
Barr Primary School, Barr

My Family

My family is here and there
They always go somewhere,
I sometimes go with them,
Conner's always on the PlayStation
Jamie's playing with his friends outside
I'm always playing with my rabbit
Mum and Dad are paragliding
On a hill today.

Heather Lorimer (7)
Barr Primary School, Barr

Animals

I love animals very much
They are good at sniffing for food
Frogs like jumping on rocks
Rabbits like running in gardens
Hedgehogs have very big spikes.

James White (7)
Barr Primary School, Barr

My Brother

My brother
He looks like a king
His hands are like the smoothest silk
His face is like a cushion
His eyes are like two balls
My brother's clothes are smart
He moves like a runner
He walks like a bear
He runs like a tiger
My brother thinks fast
I think my brother's the best.

Joe Adams (8)
Barr Primary School, Barr

Summer

This is our summer place
And the trees are green and bushy
And all the leaves are soft and smooth
And the river where we play
Is calm and gentle
The air is warm
Our voices are happy, cheerful and loud
And everything is awake.

Joanne Milroy (8)
Barr Primary School, Barr

Fire

F ire burning high
I n the dark sky
R oaring, sparkling, crackling
E nding and then dying.

Joseph Connon (7)
Barr Primary School, Barr

Pets

Pets have to go to the vets,
Small pets, tall pets,
Fat pets, skinny pets,
You get rabbits that have habits,
Pigs that always dig,
Pets, pets, pets.

I have a pet that is a dog,
He will chase a rabbit,
That is his big habit.

Jamie Lorimer (8)
Barr Primary School, Barr

Swimming

S wimming is cool
W ith lots of different strokes
I n the pool you can be free
M agical feeling flowing through your body
M illions of litres of water splashing about
I n the pool you can swim until you're wrinkled like a prune
N ow leaving the pool is the hardest thing
G oodbye pool, I will miss you, until next week.

Rebecca Watt
Barthol Chapel School, Inverurie

Recycle

R ecycle all your tins and cans
E nergy is something you can help
C ans, bottles, tins and jars
Y ou can make lots of things out of tins and cans
C ans and paper you can put into the recycling bin
L itter is not good so put it in the tip
E nergy is something you can use.

Matthew Watt (9)
Barthol Chapel School, Inverurie

Origami

Are you not allowed a pet?
Do you nag and nag and never get?
Well, here's a solution for every pet lover,
It may even suit your mother!

So grab a bit of paper
And make sure you don't caper.
For you are going to make
Something better than a cake.

An origami dog!

Fold over right,
When paper's in your sight.
Then make a triangle
But not a right angle!

And make an origami dog
That won't run off into the fog.
You won't have to pick up his mess,
Or have your sister make him a dress.

But the only problem with an origami dog
Is he likes to hog
Your desk!

Ryan Sloan (10)
Barthol Chapel School, Inverurie

LA Lakers

The Lakers, the LA Lakers, they are no fakers
They play basketball and are history makers
They can jump to the hoop and maybe the roof
They run around in yellow or blue
Faster than me or maybe you
They have players like Jordan Biggs and more
They don't dillydally,
They're focused to score.

Nathan Kirk
Barthol Chapel School, Inverurie

She

She walks on golden beaches
She walks on golden sands
But she never saw the beauty of green and blue lands
Gold, silver, diamonds, they're simply all the best
Pearls, rubies, sapphires, they're simply all the rest
She sways in golden garments
She sways in golden gowns
She walks on the sand, waves lapping around
Her suntanned heels
Her sandals crammed with shells, pearls and jewels
She walks in soft rock pools
Her hair as brown as bark on a tree
Her mouth covered by a veil
A tale of her life
Dressed in a purple sari with gold-tasselled lace on the side
She looks out to see
How she does wish she was back in that land
That green and blue land.

Mary Williams (10)
Barthol Chapel School, Inverurie

Double Trouble

D ouble trouble coming from
O ver there, I'm scared
U mbrella face
B ig foot she is
L et's walk away
E ven though I've got nowhere to go

T roubles
R ound the bench
O ver there
U nder the tree with all the
B ees
L eap to my house
E very time she comes.

Amanda Walker (11)
Barthol Chapel School, Inverurie

Who Is He?

Who is he?
He follows me
Day and night
I don't want a fight

Who is he?
As small as my knee
He's in my mind
I hope he's not mine

Who is he?
He's like a bee
He hovers over me
With a key

Who is he?
It's not just me
He tells me what's right or wrong
It just goes on and on

If you have not guessed
Your brain must be a mess

Who is he?
My conscience!

Charlotte Cooke (10)
Barthol Chapel School, Inverurie

My Birthdays

B alloons are colourful floating in the air
 I am happy, it's my special day
R eady to dance and play
T ags on my presents
H appy as can be
D ays fly by but not this one
A fter the party, it's ready for the food and cake
Y ellow candles ready for a big blow
S ausages and jelly and ice cream all for me!

Bobbie
Barthol Chapel School, Inverurie

Poor Old People

There was a girl called Adele
For the church she used to ring the bell
Until it went *boof!*
She went right through the roof
And that was the end of Adele.

There once was a lad called Tony
Who tried to ride a pony
It bucked him off
And he landed in a trough
And that was the end of poor Tony.

There once was a girl called Gail
Who was swallowed by a great big whale
She lived her life
In trouble and strife
And that's what happened to Gail.

Drew Cowie, Callum Keys & Kieran Booth (10)
Barthol Chapel School, Inverurie

My Old Friend!

My old friend, who we like to play with;
He's often associated with a type of myth.
He has a lot of arms, a hundred or so;
And lots of fingers, which hang down so low.
He's rooted to the spot, he does not go anywhere;
He does not speak, so he has no time to swear.
He reaches right up, up, up in the sky;
He's quite big, so he's not very shy.
His wrinkly, rough skin;
Is not very thin.
He's always been with me;
Guess who he is?
An old oak tree!

Jamie Strathearn (10)
Barthol Chapel School, Inverurie

Unicorn

Flying, swooping, through the air
Wings flapping without a care
Wings now dying as he comes down to land
Up, up on his back, flying through the midnight black
Soon we'll land and my journey will be over
Back to Dover, there he will land
Horn still glowing
Mane still flowing
Back to his magical land,
Unicorns dance still in a trance
In the midnight black.

Emma Simpson (9)
Barthol Chapel School, Inverurie

Gymnastics

G ymnastics is fun
Y ou've got to save your strength
M y mum coaches gymnastics
N umb body straight after
A lways on the move
S ome moves are hard and some are easy
T here are four pieces
I have skill at gymnastics
C artwheels are difficult
S pins are an easy move.

Lee-Ann Donald (11)
Barthol Chapel School, Inverurie

My Snake

I had a snake that did not bite,
But bit my friend with a fright,
It stayed outside in the cold all night.

He scared people with his tongue,
It was red, sharp and very long,
It wrapped his body around the tree,
He was friendly really, as can be!

Angus Bruce-Gardner (11)
Barthol Chapel School, Inverurie

Moving On

Moving on can be cool,
As long as it isn't moving on to a new school!
Having to start again, almost from scratch,
I feel like a stroppy teenager ready to hatch!

It's time to start to multi-task,
It's time to be myself and take off the mask,
I want to stay and I want to leave,
But I know that everyone will surely grieve!

I remember in Primary 1,
When my school years had just begun,
It was easy in Primary 1 learning how to count,
Learning why not to be a litter lout!

I've had lots of great teachers,
Seen many weird creatures,
I've learnt lots of great things over the years,
I guess what I'm trying to say,
Is thank you and cheers!

Seona Corbett (11)
Belmont Primary School, Stranraer

Moving On!

Belmont School . . . I have to leave!
On the last day we will want to grieve.
But hold your chin up high
And don't dare sigh,
At the Academy there will be work you can achieve.

Parties at the end of the year,
Everyone will scream and cheer.
The holiday season has begun,
Enjoy yourself
And have some fun.

When I start the Academy,
It will be great fun, don't you see?
Very hard the work will be.

So, there is no need to be afraid,
As long as you study hard and get a good grade.
You'll miss your old teachers and all your friends,
But you can make new ones,
Friends who will last to the very end.

Nicola Small (11)
Belmont Primary School, Stranraer

My Best Friend

My best friend is Ashley, we're both eleven,
I started hanging about with her in Primary 7,
We both have great fun,
She's quiet and I'm the loud one,
We like going down town or to the swimming pool
And I sometimes monitor with her at school,
She likes music such as Son Of Dork and McFly,
If I had to listen to that all the time, I'd die,
Because I prefer rap, hip hop and R'n'B,
We have very different tastes in music as you can see,
But I don't care, because she's a friend.

Jasmine Dickson (11)
Belmont Primary School, Stranraer

My Best Friends

My best friends are kind, caring and also sharing
When we go out to play
Everyone shouts hooray
My best friends are so cool.

My best friends are cheerful, they are also funny
They make me smile and jump up and down,
While we are down in the town.

We do lots of things together
Like go to each other's houses
We like to go swimming and do all sorts of things.

We also have sleepovers, they are fun
If I am down, they cheer me up
That is why they are my friends.

Jemma McNeillie (11)
Belmont Primary School, Stranraer

Moving On

I'm moving on,
To another school,
That place with the swimming pool,
It's going to be cool.

But I need to take it seriously,
I don't want to be bad at my work,
I need to get a good education,
In order to get a qualification.

I want to do well in mathematics,
But I don't think I'll be doing gymnastics,
I'm a little bit nervous about moving,
I really don't know what'll happen.

But I'll never forget Belmont,
The ultimate primary school,
I really don't want to leave,
It's been like a home to me.

Ross Shankly (11)
Belmont Primary School, Stranraer

Moving On

Moving on can sometimes be scary,
When you meet new people
And you go to different places,
Moving on can be scary.

I will soon be moving on,
To a place with lots of people,
It's very big, with lots of rooms,
Moving on can be scary.

I am moving to Stranraer Academy,
I am a little bit worried,
I'm not sure what teachers I will get,
Moving on can be scary.

Although I'm moving to secondary school,
I will never forget primary school,
I will never forget my teachers
And all the good times I have had.

James Caldwell (11)
Belmont Primary School, Stranraer

My School

In our class the teachers tell us we rule,
They say Belmont Primary is the best school,
We most certainly agree,
We will certainly all get a degree.

Our teachers like to yawn,
They would probably like to be mowing the garden lawn,
We all like to yap, yap, yap,
Sometimes just like a leaking tap!

The school dinners are sometimes nice,
As for the rice,
It was probably half price,
That is why my school is cool!

Kayleigh McWhirter (11)
Belmont Primary School, Stranraer

Moving On!

I am moving on into First Year
I think I should celebrate with a big cheer!

I am happy to move on
Put the past behind, it's all gone.

I want to learn more about mathematics,
Be a businessman or learn gymnastics.

I will get lots of other teachers
Some I will like, some I won't feature.

I will work hard at school
Not sit at home and play pool.

I want to be a pro-footballer
But my mum said I have to grow taller.

I hope I achieve some of these things
I will need to see what God brings.

Lewis Dunn (11)
Belmont Primary School, Stranraer

My Best Friend

Jasmine is my best friend
She's as cool as toast,
Out of all my friends
I like her the most.

The brown-eyed girl
With the short brown hair
In any game she plays fair
Tall enough to get through a game of football.

I would never just pretend
To be her friend,
Because I will be her friend
Till the end
That's my friend
Jazzy Jasmine.

Paige Castle (11)
Belmont Primary School, Stranraer

My School

My school is really cool,
My school is Belmont Primary School,
With all my friends and teachers,
They help me learn, I know that is true.

My friends are funny
Here's some of their names
Gina, Lori, Nicola Reay, Emma and Jasmine too,
They all are nice and give advice too.

Our teacher, Mrs Neil and our head teacher, Mr Burns
Are really nice
They help me be louder and now I'm confident
No matter what I do
So that's my opinion
Of Belmont Primary School
Just remember that we rule!

Ashley Hughes (11)
Belmont Primary School, Stranraer

My Best Friends

I've got lots of
Best friends

My best friends
Brighten me up
When I am down

We go swimming
Have fun
And splash around

The best thing is
They don't
Let you down

You can tell them secrets
You know they won't tell
That's what friendship's all about!

Rachel McCormick (11)
Belmont Primary School, Stranraer

My School

In our school I can tell we rule!
We beat other people
From all the different schools.

Our school is called Belmont Primary
It is the best school ever
Because Mr Burns and all the other teachers
Are very cool!

Every other school
Really doesn't rule
Because everyone knows
We are cool!

And as for Mrs Neil
She can rule
Because she is the coolest
Of the cool!

Gina Louise Ellis (11)
Belmont Primary School, Stranraer

My School

My school is cool,
The teachers are nice,
They give us lots of advice.

Mrs Neil likes us
Whatever we do
And Mr Burns does too.

Mr Burns is kind
Alexandra is too
She's my favourite P3
Because she's always kind to me.

The P7s are cool
They say we rule the school
And I love
Belmont Primary School.

Nicola Reay (11)
Belmont Primary School, Stranraer

My Best Friend

My best friend is caring
She is sharing and kind
We always go swimming or down to town
Have sleepovers and prat around

We always have fun
Laugh and run
We have the same colour hair
And we make everything fair

If I am upset
She will always make me better
When I go to her house
She is as quiet as a mouse.

Charlene (11)
Belmont Primary School, Stranraer

My School

My school is cool,
It is Belmont Primary School,
My friends are fun,
They like to run,
The teachers are nice
And give us advice,
In my school it is the best!

In our class we always work,
Especially when we're doing maths,
We all are friendly and never bully,
In my school we rule!

The school dinners are mostly nice,
With our chicken curry and rice,
Our head teacher hardly shouts,
He's always nice and never cruel,
I will never forget my cool school!

Lori Moore (11)
Belmont Primary School, Stranraer

Moving On

I am moving on to First Year,
Now it is time to cheer,
To Stranraer Academy,
To work really hard.

Listening really closely to the teachers,
The teachers could be good or bad,
They could scare me a little bit,
I am so excited.

Meet different people and old friends,
Starting all over again,
I hope my education doesn't end,
I'll get right to the end.

Lots of brilliant new subjects
And new classrooms
Maybe I'll get lost
Someone please help me!

I want a good education
And to get a qualification
I will really stick at it
And do my very best.

Time to move on,
Time to go away.

Emma Breadon (11)
Belmont Primary School, Stranraer

Moving On

I'm going to the Academy,
I'm feeling very nervous,
I wonder if my form teacher will be nice
Or strict with lots of rules?

I hope I meet new friends,
To replace my old ones that have gone,
I hope they're funny and friendly,
Or cool with lots of humour.

I wonder what subjects,
I will have to learn this year,
Boring old French, or super science,
I can't wait to learn them all!

I really want to learn this year
And get a good education,
So that when I leave the school,
I can get a qualification.

I've got a feeling that this year,
Will be a year to remember,
Because this year
I start to fulfil my ambition!

John Dalrymple (11)
Belmont Primary School, Stranraer

Moving On

I'm moving on
I'm going on
Leaving the past behind me
I'm so excited about
The Academy

I hope the fun
Has just begun
For I can't wait
For the future to come

The teachers could be good
The teachers could be bad
So I hope they're not in a bad mood
So they're really, *really* bad

I always try my best
At every single test
To get good grades
So I can be praised

I could get lost
Or even get bossed
I could get detention
Or even a suspension

Even though I'm moving on
I will never forget Belmont.

Scott Gibson (11)
Belmont Primary School, Stranraer

My Best Friend

My best friend is Rachael
She lives just down the road
She's cool and caring
And really sharing.

Rachael is a kind person
And also really funny
She makes me smile all the time
I really like her character.

If I'm down
She always cheers me up
We do lots of things
Like the Guides and Majorettes.

We sometimes have tea
At each other's houses
We have sleepovers
That are cool.

I'm really pleased
I have a friend
Who is really kind
I'm glad to have a friend like Rachael.

Rebecca Hannah (11)
Belmont Primary School, Stranraer

Moving On

I'm moving on
The old school gone
I'm really excited, but a bit sad
My head is spinning, it's all going mad!

In primary school I've seen all there is to be seen
To be moving on I am very keen
I really want to learn about maths
And maybe open some new and exciting career paths.

I can't wait until it all starts
To be doing English, PE and the exciting world of art
I'll try and work hard at school
And not sit around trying to be cool!

I really want to be a nurse
And put some money in my purse
I want to meet new friends, but not to leave my old ones behind
To meet new friends that are happy and kind.

Oh, what a year it is going to be
A lot of things to do and see
There have been happy memories and sad ones too
But I'll always remember the memories with *you!*

Laura Casey (11)
Belmont Primary School, Stranraer

Moving On!

I can't wait till I leave this school
Although I think it's fun and cool
It's time to go, I'm moving on
When summertime comes, I'll be gone.

I'm going into First Year
Everyone's going to shout and cheer
I'm looking forward to meeting new friends
Although my love for Belmont will never end.

I want to pass my tests
And be one of the best
I want a really good job
Rather than sitting at home, being a slob!

I've had lots of laughs at this school
And I've hardly ever broken a rule
I've really enjoyed being at Belmont
And I know one thing for sure,
I'll be crying when I leave!

Louise Connor (11)
Belmont Primary School, Stranraer

Who Am I?

I am dark aqua-blue,
I wriggle and giggle when I get tickled,
I go with the flow,
I like spring,
All the baby ducks and swans come and learn on me,
I am a bit wide and a bit deep,
I am soft,
I run through your hands,
Who am I?

I am a stream.

Amy Barbour (11)
Bervie Primary School, Inverbervie

Who Am I?

I am large, old and wise
To climb me, I would not advise
You can find me in a park
Tall, still and covered in bark.

My bark is dark and my leaves are green
And I like to keep myself quite clean
Standing still for hundreds of years
Standing there, fear from fears.

I love it in the summer sun
It is always so much fun
Seeing all the children play
It's a pity they can't stay
Who am I?

I am a tree.

Amy Shand (11)
Bervie Primary School, Inverbervie

Who Am I?

I'm grey and flat,
I'm shaped as a rectangle and I'm long,
I'm a playful person and I like to laugh,
I'm a gossipy person,
I like the children playing on me,
But when they go home, I'm by myself.

I don't like people dropping their litter on me,
Then I get angry,
I like summer because they play on me,
I don't like winter, because they can't play on me
Because it's icy,
Who am I?

I'm a playground.

Kirsty Archibald (11)
Bervie Primary School, Inverbervie

Who Am I?

I'm long and thin,
With a knobbly chin,
The children play,
Every day,
On me which I enjoy,
They use me instead of a toy.

I'm brown and green,
But certainly not mean,
I love a little sing-song,
When I hear church bells go *ding-dong*.

I have been living for about ten years,
I can hear you with my big ears,
A child is my best friend,
Though they tend to drive me round the bend.

All the birds love to sit on me,
Who am I?

I am a tree.

Rachel Criggie (11)
Bervie Primary School, Inverbervie

My Eyes

My eyes are blue, brown and grey
My eyes are as grey as Alex's pencil
And as grey as old people's hair.
My eyes are like no one else's, so I like them
My eyes are as blue as the B on the Celebrations box
Full of sugary sweets.
My eyes are as brown as a rusty train track
That has sat there for a billion years.

Michael Anderson (11)
Bervie Primary School, Inverbervie

Who Am I?

I am the thing that is covered in rocks
I have been here since the first ice age
I have a cold peak that no one has reached
My colour is dark brown
I have a deep and grumbling voice
I hate it when people drop litter on me in the summer
I like to have a little bit of company
But not a lot
Who am I?

I am a mountain.

Kyle Leslie (11)
Bervie Primary School, Inverbervie

My Eyes

My eyes are like glittering rubies
And are as blue as the sky
Blue like a summer sea
It's as if they are as shiny as a diamond.

Nathaneal Wilson (11)
Bervie Primary School, Inverbervie

My Eyes

My eyes are as green as the grass on a hot day,
They are as green as a leaf.
My eyes are as brown as a golden eagle's feathers,
They have a hint of gold which is as gold as the sun.
My eyes are as green as a frog,
They are as green as the carpet below me.
They are as brown as my hair,
They are mine.

Alex Scott (11)
Bervie Primary School, Inverbervie

Cherry Blossom - Haikus

The flowers blossom
I see beautiful, blue birds
And it feels magic.

Rosy-pink stands out
It catches my eye with fun
It now feels alive.

They sing with laughter
They feel willing and ready
They dance all day long.

Joanne Stirling (11)
Bervie Primary School, Inverbervie

The Sea

The wind, blowing like a whistle,
The waves, crashing like a car,
The lightning, flashing like a torch,
The sea, hissing like a snake
The thunder, banging like knocking,
The spray, spraying like polish,
The wind, wailing like a whale,
The waves, punching like boxers.

Ryan Stewart (11)
Bervie Primary School, Inverbervie

My Eyes

My eyes are as green as grass
As shiny as the sun
As green as a leaf in the summer
As bloodshot as if they were covered in blood
They are as green as an alien.

Josh Filson (11)
Bervie Primary School, Inverbervie

War

I look up to the starry sky
Before
The air raid siren blares full blast.
People run, scream and shout,
Everywhere I look, there's chaos
And then the bombers strike.
Flames burst into the sky,
Changing the dark blue night to light,
The air raid shelters packed full with people
And then there's calm.
The all-clear siren goes, to great relief,
But tragic losses tense the atmosphere.

Alexander Jones (11)
Bervie Primary School, Inverbervie

As They Notice - Haiku

As people notice
The pink cherry blossom as
The people go watch.

Krysta Stewart (11)
Bervie Primary School, Inverbervie

The Sound Of War

The sound of war is not peaceful,
Guns being fired and sirens wailing,
It's not the place to be.
People screaming, bombs exploding,
It's not a safe place to be.
Children crying their hearts out, because they're frightened,
Air raid wardens shouting at people, so they can hurry up.
After a while, the bombs are gone
And in the end, there is a cheer!

Blair Stephen (10)
Bervie Primary School, Inverbervie

The Sea

The seagulls were squealing like a baby crying,
The sea was foaming like beer.
The buoys were bobbing like a boat,
The waves were smashing against the shore like a hammer to a brick.
The strong wind was bashing like giants playing skittles,
The wind was whistling like a dog whistle.
The waves were thundering like God moving his furniture,
The water was as wet as a swimming pool
And
The air was as grey as an old school uniform.

Daniel Lovick (11)
Bervie Primary School, Inverbervie

The Sea

The wind screeched like a banshee
And waves rose up like wild stallions leaping over the world.
Rain fell like sapphires out of a jewellery box
And thunder crashed like Death's horse's hoof beats.
Boats were tossed effortlessly, as if thrown by a giant hand
And lightning streaked across the sky, like a golden shooting star.

Scott Dow (11)
Bervie Primary School, Inverbervie

Cheerfulness

Cheerfulness is yellow
It tastes like a jam sandwich
It smells like lavender
And it looks like the sun on a nice day
It sounds like a river flowing
Cheerfulness feels like a walk in the park.

Stuart Lownie (10)
Bervie Primary School, Inverbervie

The Blitz

People screaming, children crying,
Shells screeching,
Bombs falling.
People rushing around,
Planes flying.
Tanks rattling and rumbling,
Doodlebugs exploding.
The siren wailing,
The horrible smell of gunpowder
And the smell of rubber gas masks.
Machine guns firing at the planes,
Houses burning and crackling,
These are the things that happen in the war.

Ailish Lyall (10)
Bervie Primary School, Inverbervie

Anger

Anger is black
It tastes like dark, dark chocolate
It smells like a burnt rose
It looks like a dark black coat
It sounds like a dark, loud, banging noise
It feels like I never want to be angry again.

Lesa Galloway (10)
Bervie Primary School, Inverbervie

Happiness

Happiness is yellow
It tastes like sweets
And it smells like flowers
Happiness looks like an open field with birds
And sounds like grass flowing in the wind
Happiness feels nice in my stomach.

Martyn Horner (10)
Bervie Primary School, Inverbervie

Sights Of War

Sights before:
Before the bombing raids started
You could see children playing, laughing, having fun,
The houses standing proud and tall,
The sun shining in the clear blue sky.

Sights after:
After the bombing raids had finished,
You could see the sadness in people's eyes,
Rubble on the roads,
People scampering around,
Trying to find injured friends and family,
Exploded and unexploded shells on the ground,
The Germans had made a big mess.

Paige Lamont (10)
Bervie Primary School, Inverbervie

Love

Love is pink
It tastes like chocolate
It smells like roses
It looks like hearts
It sounds like birds singing
It feels like you're in Heaven.

Samantha Wood (10)
Bervie Primary School, Inverbervie

The Horrors Of War

It all started when I was in bed,
The siren wailed,
Everyone was running to the shelter,
Or to help someone injured.
I ran to my shelter,
I heard a bang.

I was worried,
I thought it was my house,
The all clear was great,
But unfortunately,
My house was
Bombed!

Corey Fowler (10)
Bervie Primary School, Inverbervie

Pride

Pride is yellow
It tastes like a bar of Turkish delight
And smells like cappuccino
Pride looks like a hundred bars of gold
And it sounds like an orchestra
Pride feels like drinking hot chocolate on a snowy day.

Callum Clark (10)
Bervie Primary School, Inverbervie

The Blitz

The air raid siren started to wail
There were people rushing around everywhere
I started to get worried,
I ran to the shelter as quickly as I could, with my family.
We made it to the shelter,
Just before the bombs started to drop.
I heard banging, smashing and exploding,
I could smell burning and gunpowder.
I felt angry, annoyed, scared,
People started to sing and I joined in,
It calmed me down and I forgot about the war.
Then the all-clear siren wailed,
I walked out of the shelter,
Our house was alright,
I felt relieved,
But I knew I would have to do this all over again.

Cameron Donaldson (11)
Bervie Primary School, Inverbervie

Joy

Joy is pink
It tastes like strawberries
And smells like chocolate
Joy looks like a plate of jelly
And sounds like people running around, playing
Joy feels like a hot drink running down your throat.

Kyle Casson (10)
Bervie Primary School, Inverbervie

The Blitz

The Blitz is a very depressing time,
But when the all-clear siren goes off, everything is fine.
People shoving, pushing and crying,
Bombs dropping, screaming and exploding.
When the siren goes off, I put my gas mask on,
It go outside and all of the houses are gone.
I am anxious, worried and scared,
All the animals are terrified and fearful.
I'm lost and I don't know what to do,
I'm trying to find my parents,
But I haven't got a clue.
Suddenly, the all-clear siren goes off,
Everyone takes off their gas masks
And has a little cough.
I finally find my parents and everyone is fine,
We try to get back to normal after a very long time.

Holly Donald (10)
Bervie Primary School, Inverbervie

Fear

Fear is black
It tastes like a scary type of drug
It smells like a drop of blood
It sounds like a loud scream
It feels like a knife sticking in your chest.

Daniel Bland (10)
Bervie Primary School, Inverbervie

The Bitterness Of The Blitz

The siren begins to moan,
The rush of footsteps head to the shelters.
The bombing begins.
I hear the screaming of the innocent people and worry,
In my shelter, I panic,
As my neighbour's house begins to burn.
I see the shell with my own two eyes
And hear the crackling of the fire,
I begin to worry.
Suddenly, rubble drops from my house,
I shriek and scream as I hear the rubble clang against my shelter,
I fear for my life, it may end soon.
The wafts of smoke do not help me,
Especially now my house is burning.
The all clear goes off, but what do I care?
My house is burning down and I can't stay with my neighbours,
I guess I'm just going to wait and see,
What horrid future awaits me.

Calum Tait (10)
Bervie Primary School, Inverbervie

Machines

M is for a mighty machine working on the building site
A is for an ambulance, white and fast
C is for a coal lorry working hard
H is for a helicopter flying high in the sky
I is for the in-shore lifeboat, small and fast
N is for Nuffield, a tractor working in the field
E is for excavator, digging up the ground
S is for spinning machine, spinning all day.

Andrew Floydd (11)
Brora Primary School, Brora

Happiness

Happiness makes me feel good
Happiness is a steaming hot chocolate
Happiness is when snow falls
Happiness is good humoured
Happiness is a birthday
Happiness is when you're given presents on Christmas Day
Happiness is cheerful
Happiness is when your favourite football team wins the cup
Happiness is a cold snowman
Happiness is making a new friend
Happiness is glad
Happiness is delighted
Happiness is swimming in the sea on a hot day
Happiness is your birthday
Happiness is simply the best!

Liam Sutherland (11)
Brora Primary School, Brora

Autumn

Leaves of all colours
Floating in the breeze
Rustling down that road
That road of memories

Trees follow that road
Waving their bare branches as we walk by
The sunlight rains down on those beams
Waiting for the green leaves of spring to arrive

But these days are not for long
Winter will soon come
Snow, hail and ice
It will come at a price

Another month of patiently waiting
For those green leaves.

Jennifer Robertson (11)
Brora Primary School, Brora

Winter

Winter brings lots of snow
Children's cheeks full of glow.
Winter winds passing by
Clouds flying very high.

The winter winds blow
People's faces start to glow
The rivers are in full flow.

Duck ponds frozen over
Children skating all over.
Red berries on the holly
Making you feel very jolly.

Snowflakes falling down
Roads are white all around the town.
Winter is cold
And it is time for the scarf to unfold.

The daytime brings snowball fights
Stars shine brightly at night.

Snowmen standing tall and bright
Shining in the winter light.

Winter is here again.

Carl Anderson (11)
Brora Primary School, Brora

Foxes

Foxes sneaking around day and night
If you catch them, they might bite
I've never seen them growl before
If I do they might *roar*
I have seen a fox before
In a forest with its cubs
When I saw them, I was happy to see them play together
And now I wish they were mine.

Heather Carter (11)
Brora Primary School, Brora

River

A river is longer than Rapunzel's hair
As soft as a cloud
And the colour of the sky on a clear day
As cool as a soothing breeze
It is as warm as the swimming pool
I like rivers, I hope you do too.

They are fun to swim in, play in, sail in
Fish in, dive in, canoe in, snorkel in
Wash filthy clothes in
And wash dirty dishes in.

Rivers flow all around the world
They flow into the sea
And they travel
All over the world.

Andrew Sutherland (11)
Brora Primary School, Brora

Stressed

I feel stressed when
I keep getting my maths wrong
Stressed makes me feel upset
Being stressed is like a big red devil
Stressed makes me feel unconfident about myself
Stressed is when there is too much going on
Stressed makes me feel scared and left out
Stressed is a volcano erupting
Stressed makes me feel like a one-year-old
Stressed is when I can't sleep at night
Stressed is when there is too much pressure
Stressed is like a bulldog on a bad day
Stressed makes me want to curl up into a corner and never come out
Stressed is when I get nothing, no matter what
A calming breath will blow away
The negative feeling of a stressful day.

Lauren Miller (11)
Brora Primary School, Brora

War

A first shot starts a hard, long war
The darkness clouds in like dark skies
Men, women and children die in innocence
Alas, enemies and neutral soldiers destroying everyone

Gun-firing over the hills, knowing people are dying
Dads, grandads, teens and kids in the war
The sadness just seems to drag on and on
People getting lonelier and angrier than ever

The jets fly overhead dropping bombs
The tanks smash and destroy everything in the way
Machine guns, grenades and rockets killing
Like an acid flood all over the world

The prison camps are dark and dusty
But their freedom is drawing nearer
The sun manages to get through
And the war is finally over

So this war ends, years later than it started
And there will soon be another
But the people will never forget this
And the people who died will be remembered forever.

Sol Campbell (11)
Brora Primary School, Brora

Happiness

H appy is when I feel free
A mong the lovely field, full of beautiful flowers
P eople are nice to you, so be nice to them
P opcorn makes my senses jumpy
I mpossible gives me a sense of helplessness
N ice friends make me welcome at school
E asy makes me feel my work is simple
S mart makes me feel serious
S unset makes me feel safe.

Sophie Taylor (11)
Brora Primary School, Brora

Excitement

Feelings of excitement overpower me
Excitement is when I watch TV
It's like when nerves shoot through you
It is like the 'Supercalafragalisticexpealidotious' song
Excitement is like a new car
It is like when you get something you really want
Excitement is climbing a tree
It is like my PS2
Excitement is like successfully doing a trick on a BMX
It is when you're meeting your friend
It is when you roll in the grass
It is like a dream
Excitement is when I'm with my dad
It is when you're going on holiday
My family is full of excitement.

Allen Martin (11)
Brora Primary School, Brora

Happiness

Happiness is like swimming with dolphins
Happiness was when I got a 12ft pool for my birthday
Happiness is like a sun shining down
Being cheerful is when I go abroad
Happiness is like when I see spring flowers on a winter's day
Being jolly is when I open a big present for Christmas
And in it there's an electric scooter
Gleeful is seeing the sunset over the deep blue sea
Merriment is seeing a shooting star to make a wish
Cheerfulness is when you go out for a walk with your family
Happiness is a cheese sandwich melted in the microwave
Happiness is hearing people's laughter
But most of all, happiness is being content with what you have.

Lois Colvin (11)
Brora Primary School, Brora

Rally Day

Rally day is such fun
I come in a transit with my car on the back
I look around
There are Audis to Subarus waiting to race
And a land rover is waiting impatiently.

We get the car off the trailer
We get the car started
And drive it up to the starting line
We wait for the three second countdown
And when the buzzer goes
We are off like a rocket.
Every checkpoint we pass we give a sigh of relief
The finish is in sight
We go for the finish
And we dodge anything in our way
We wait for the results
And we've come second
There is always next year to come first
We think to ourselves.

Euan Cameron (11)
Brora Primary School, Brora

Boldness

Boldness is like when I stand up for what I believe in
A soldier standing against an army of hundreds of other soldiers
Being top of a business
And fighting to keep my title.
They think they are the bee's knees
But they could not be any more saucy than me
Cocky businessmen coming to your door
Trying to sell you an iron or double glazing
When you don't need it
Boldness is something children don't have these days.

Mark David Keith (11)
Brora Primary School, Brora

Cars

F is for Ford, cool as can be and beautiful
A is for Austin Mini, small and old as can be, like a rusty old gate
S is for Subaru, fast and nice, noisy and new
T is for Toyota, good for cornering, not fast

C is for Corvette, nice and small
A is for Aston Martin, smells like roses
R is for Rover, big and small, shiny and dirty
S is for Smart car, small but not comfy

A is for Astra, fast and attractive
R is for Renault Clio, slow and no space
E is for Escort, cheap and cheerful

G is for Golf, old and scabby
O is for Orion, saucy and hot
O is for Opal Manta, fast and smelly
D is for Daf, as old as can be, as silly as a clown.

Connor Simmonds (11)
Brora Primary School, Brora

Birds

Flying so quickly
Yet so quietly
Sing like angels
On a sunny winter morning.

Birds are like clouds
So swift but silent
Sitting waiting for old ladies
To throw bread
When they have eaten
They are back on their big journey.

Birds, they are all different
They are so free
They have not a care in the world
Until springtime comes round again.

Jack McNee (11)
Brora Primary School, Brora

A Poem About My Dog

My dog Jasper
Is a golden retriever
He's large and furry
His colour is gold
But he isn't very bold.

He's so friendly
And rather lazy
Loves my friends
As he goes crazy
Getting excited
Wanting to join in
With any game we play.

He loves his toys
Cuddles and plays with them
He's just a silly boy.

My dog Jasper
You have to love him
Cos he's so cute and funny
He even plays with my bunny
And she's called Abby
They're so happy.

Samantha Clack (11)
Brora Primary School, Brora

Sad

Sad is a waterfall rushing down,
People are making fun of you
Upset is a face turned downwards
To curl up and die.
I get annoyed and called names
Miserable is a volcano erupting
Lower than the deep blue sea
Gloomy as the stormy night.

Jodie Grant (11)
Brora Primary School, Brora

The Days Of Seasons

Today is winter
The bulbs lay low
All sleeps in the garden
Covered by a duvet of snow

The snowdrops awaken
Drawn by the light
Pushing their way
To join spring's delights

Days are lengthening
Summer is here
As to my window
A climbing rose appears

The flowers are fading
Gusts of wind chase the leaves overhead
Tools are put past
In the garden shed

We plant the winter crocus
And pray the season will be short
Remembering that the cycle continues
As our teacher has taught.

Ruth Liddell (11)
Brora Primary School, Brora

Excited

Excited is when I get a new toy
Excited makes me restless
Like the night before Christmas
Excited like a soldier coming
Home from the war
Excited is like going on holiday
To a really hot place
Excited is when you are thrilled
Like going to play golf or football.

Stuart Campbell (11)
Brora Primary School, Brora

The Old Man

There was an old man from Ayr
Who liked to eat lots of pears
He went to the shop
To buy a big mop
And then got chased by a big fat bear.

Bruce Sutherland (11)
Brora Primary School, Brora

Shark

S wimming slowly in the cold sea
H idden turtle in the coral reef below
A ngry shark swimming closer
R eady to attack with his ginormous teeth
K ills the turtle - *snap!*

Jamie Clark (10)
Campie Primary School, Musselburgh

Marathon

You're at the start,
Your heart is beating,
There is no room for cheating,
You start,
Ten kilometres gone,
People cheer you on,
You look at your watch,
That puts joy in your heart,
Your legs tire,
You try to get as much air as you can,
Then you see it,
The finish line.

Euan Shedden (10)
Carolside Primary School, Clarkston

A Killer Snake

There was a snake in the tall grass,
He is always waiting for prey to pass,
When he finds someone, he jumps out,
But the people always begin to shout.

He can squeeze you tight,
But watch out, he might bite,
He can burst the tyre of your bike,
With only one big strike.

He can kill you,
But not a kangaroo,
He can give you a nasty bite,
But he can also destroy your kite.

He likes eating things twice,
Because he thinks they are very nice,
He hates rice,
But he can break a dice.

Lewis MacLeod (8)
Carolside Primary School, Clarkston

War

Nobody likes war
It goes on and on
The scream of the air raid siren
And having to run to the shelter
Boom!
The bombs deafen you.

Everybody dreads the letter
Saying your husband's dead
The pain and suffering still goes on
Nobody likes war
It goes on and on.

Lorna Beattie (10)
Carolside Primary School, Clarkston

My Garden

My garden's not big and my garden's not small
But I know it is not as big as the mall
There's a wall at the front and a hedge at the back
And in the middle, there's a huge, big, brown soil sack.

Up at the top, there's a big, red shed
And also the ants have a cosy little bed
There's Dad's tools in there and also my bike
And I have three sledges, but there's only one that I like.

The path from the front leads straight to the door
Cutting the grass is a really big chore
My car's at the side, it's red and it's fast
If it's on the motorway, you'll never get past.

Up at the top, there's a little bird house
Who could fit in there? Not even a mouse
Has it got a mini television and a kitchen too
I wonder what it's like in there, don't you?

Amanda Carlin (10)
Carolside Primary School, Clarkston

Oh Scotland

Oh Scotland, with your hills so wide
Your grass so green
And your trees so tall
Why do we pollute you with gas and steam?

Oh Scotland, with your buildings so high
Your animals so small
And your children so bright
Why do we spoil you with graffiti and fights?

Oh Scotland, can we change our ways?
Your seas are so blue
And your land is so green
Why do we damage you?

Rachel Hannah (10)
Carolside Primary School, Clarkston

Bullying

Bullying is a naughty thing to do,
Oh no, what to do?
Carolside is as happy as can be,
That's why we are bully free.

If bullies are not nice,
Just feed them to the mice,
It can make people very sad
And sometimes very mad.

It is very black and dull,
That's why it hurts the skull,
Just be nice,
Don't think twice.

Stop bullying, follow the code,
Or you'll turn into a big fat toad,
Just throw them out of your mind
And all the bullies will rewind.

Clare MacLeod (8)
Carolside Primary School, Clarkston

Imagine A . . .

Imagine a cat knitting a mat
Imagine a dog lost in the fog
Imagine a fish eating out of a dish
Imagine a pig throwing a twig
Imagine a sheep in bed, fast asleep
Imagine a bird speaking a word
Imagine a bunny trying to eat honey
Imagine a lion sitting and crying
But most of all
Imagine you
Being stuck in a zoo.

Amy Johnston (10)
Carolside Primary School, Clarkston

Miss Moss - My Teacher

My teacher has nice hair
But she is like a big teddy bear
My teacher is very thin
It looks like her legs are made out of tin
My teacher, she is very good at maths
But she never lets anyone pass
My teacher, she is called Miss Moss
She thinks that she is the boss
My teacher is kind
But some people think she is blind
My teacher has good fashion sense
It must cost a lot of pence
My teacher went on a date
I think it is her lifelong mate
My teacher's garden has got nice flowers
I think she has got magic gardening powers.

Jemma Blanchflower (11)
Carolside Primary School, Clarkston

Usher

Usher is a crusher
He wears a lot of blusher
He goes to the mall
To make a phone call

He thinks he is so cool
But he is a bit of a fool
He turns up late
Because he was on a date

To get all the girls
He loves to give them pearls
The girls scream
Because they think they're in a dream.

Aniket Kumar (10)
Carolside Primary School, Clarkston

My Class

I go to school in Clarkston town
Callum, Craig and Ryan are the class clowns.
I am in the best class - 7C
At break, my teachers go for a cup of tea.

In my class we have our own TV
Four girls are known as the Famous Four
Kirsten, Sarah, Aimee and me.
Mark and Cameron are cheeky to the teacher
Karen and Laura write good stories
About mystical creatures.

My class is certainly not a bore
So you'd better not have a lay down
And go for a nice wee snore!

Cara Sneddon (11)
Carolside Primary School, Clarkston

Food

It smelt so good,
My brother was so rude,
He picked it up and threw it,
He definitely smacked it.

My friend came in
And he gave a big grin,
Who wants to eat,
Lots of meat.

The pizza was yummy,
My tummy was scrummy,
I loved it so much,
That I needed a crutch.

Let's have one more thing to eat,
Do you want more meat?
My friend was Ross,
He thought he was the boss.

Andrew Warnock (8)
Carolside Primary School, Clarkston

The Bottle Of Pop

One day I went to the shop
To buy a bottle of pop.
I opened the pop
Then there was a knock.

I went to the knock
I didn't see the lock.
Then I went for a walk
Then I saw a shuttlecock.

I got my bottle of pop
I wanted to hop.
I bought a mop
I bought the mop from the shop.

I got my pop
From the shop.
I opened it
And a fire lit.

It burnt my pop
I heard the knock.
Then I saw the lock
And got a new bottle of pop.

Callum Tarvit (8)
Carolside Primary School, Clarkston

Grandpa

My grandpa can be funny
Well, sometimes he can be
All the stories he tells us
Interest me
My grandpa is a friendly grandpa
To my brother, sister and me
My grandpa is an intelligent grandpa
That I can see
My grandpa is a healthy grandpa
Because he drinks a lot of green tea.

Ross Landsburgh (11)
Carolside Primary School, Clarkston

Shark

I have a shark called Jaws
And he made up the laws
He eats meat
And he loves the heat.

He has a white body
And he likes Noddy
He eats fish
In a dish.

He lives in the sea
And tries to eat me
He likes me
And he likes to pee.

He has a friend called Nipper
And he likes to call him Pipper
He went to William Wood High
And one of his friends died.

He knows Tigger
And he is a digger
He ate a snail
Which left a trail.

Jordan Black (8)
Carolside Primary School, Clarkston

A Fairy Ball

A fairy was wearing a leaf dress
It was in such a mess
Down came her daughter
With a glass of water

Her dress was made of silk
Her mum dropped her milk
'That dress is so nice,'
Said the little mice

They went to a grand ball
Which was in a mall
It was very late at night
But it was still bright

There was a disco light
And it was very bright
Then they went home
To their house in Rome

She was crowned fairy dancer
With her mum Prancer
Then they watched the news
They were very confused.

Fiona Clyde (8)
Carolside Primary School, Clarkston

The Shop

One sunny day I went to a shop,
To buy bottles of fizzy pop,
I drank every single one
Then there were none.

Another day, I went back to the shop,
To buy a crop,
To set up a scene,
In front of a teen.

Another day, I went back to the shop,
To buy a mop,
To clean the floor,
Then the door.

Another day, I was going to the shop
When I saw a cop,
I saw a car
And people going to a bar.

One day I went to the shop,
To buy a top,
It was a size three,
It did not fit me.

Laura Forbes (8)
Carolside Primary School, Clarkston

Being Bullied

I used to get bullied
Because I wasn't cool
I'd wake up in the morning
And dread going to school

It's time for a change
Clothes and personality
So sit back and concentrate
As you read my reality

If I was a Goth
I'd have long black hair
My face would be white
And my eyes would always stare

If I was a ned
I'd skive off school
I'd go to the swimming pool
And act very cool

If I was posh
I'd have lots of dosh
I would live in a castle
Life wouldn't be a hassle

But then I thought, no
I don't need to change
I don't have a problem
But the bullies do!

Aimee McKinven (11)
Carolside Primary School, Clarkston

A Bright Day

The day begins with the sun
And is not the only one.
Slowly stretching up and out,
Spreading light around and about.
Down the mountains above the trees,
Making them rustle with the little breeze.

A trip to the beach,
With plenty of sun.
Blending into the water
And making a band.
The ocean and sea,
Pushing and crashing into each other,
Waving it over and over again.

The end of the day nears,
Tucking the sun into the Earth,
Making way for the moon and stars.

Humza Ismail (11)
Carolside Primary School, Clarkston

Football Is My Hobby

Football is my hobby, I play it every day
I meet up with my friends and then we go and play
Football is my hobby, I play it in the park
And if I am allowed, I can stay there till it's dark
Football is my hobby and I like the tricks
Kicking the ball and all the fancy flicks
Football is my hobby and I play for a team
Playing for Celtic is my biggest dream
Football is my hobby, it is fun to play
I like to play football every day
Football is my hobby, I let everyone play
If everyone enjoys it?
I cannot say.

Craig O'Brien (11)
Carolside Primary School, Clarkston

My Dog Sasha

My dog Sasha is the best
She is better than all the rest
She runs in the park
Then eats her bone
And after she sleeps on her own
She once ate a firework on Bonfire Night
That gave my family a fright
But thankfully, she slept all night
We did not expect she would do such a thing
But I suppose dogs will do anything
And sometimes she runs away
Once she ran so far away
She was missing for almost a day
We found her in another street
In a garden with lots to eat
So that's Sasha's story
I won't go on and bore you
But spare some thoughts
When you see a dog with lots of spots
Ask yourself, is that Sasha before you?

Cameron Reid (11)
Carolside Primary School, Clarkston

My Guinea Pig

M unching
Y oung

G orgeous
U naware
I ncredible
N aughty
E ager
A dorable

P retty
I nteresting
G uinea pig.

Christopher Anderson (11)
Carolside Primary School, Clarkston

The Child Of Morning

Dawn, the child of morning, rises
Early every single day
Her glowing touch
Lights up the world

Dawn, the child of morning, wakes up
Every sleeping flower and plant
Her weather power decides
If today is sunny or wet

Then Dawn, child of morning
Passes onto Star, child of night
Who darkens the sky
And spreads sleeping dust over everything

Star, child of night, makes
Sure everyone's asleep before
Dawn, child of morning
Takes over for the next day.

Laura McAughtrie (11)
Carolside Primary School, Clarkston

Dogs

Dogs can be big
Dogs can be small
Dogs can be thin
Dogs can be tall
Dogs can be white, brown or black
Dogs can be fierce and attack
Dogs can be nice and sit on your lap
Dogs can be evil and eat all your snacks
Dogs can be fun, others go runs
Dogs wag their tails
Dogs can just wail
Dogs go to the park
Dogs love to bark
Which is the dog for you?

Ryan Bell (11)
Carolside Primary School, Clarkston

Chocolate

Chocolate is my favourite sweet
Chocolate is what I like to eat
Chocolate ice cream, chocolate cakes
Chocolate biscuits that you can bake.
Hot chocolate with tasty bits
When it's hot, it stings my lips
Chocolate that is nice and sweet
That's what I like for a treat!
I like chocolate because it's yummy
If I don't eat chocolate, my stomach feels funny!
Chocolate comes in different sizes
Big, medium and small
There are lots of types of chocolate
But I like them all!
Too much chocolate can make you sick
I don't care, because it makes me tick
I like all chocolate, I can't really pick!

Maaria Zabir (11)
Carolside Primary School, Clarkston

Untitled

W ell, you are here, now come in
E nter our house
L et's go inside
C ome in, follow me
O ur guest has arrived, I'll show him around
M ake yourself at home
E at what you like

C lean your shoes
O ur guest is happy
M eet our guest
E at anything

I will see you again
N ice to meet you.

Waqas Hussain (11)
Carolside Primary School, Clarkston

Feelings

Feelings can be good
Feelings can be bad
Happiness is like yellow
It can make you feel all mellow
Sadness is like grey
When you've had a really tough day
Anger is like red
With everything boiling up inside your head
Shyness is like pink
You might be shy if you get a wink
These are just some feelings you may have
There is jealousy, excitement
Or you might be bored
These are just some feelings
There are lots, lots more.

Sarah Beattie (11)
Carolside Primary School, Clarkston

Gerbils

Gerbils can be big
Gerbils can be small
Gerbils can really be any size at all
Some gerbils are white
They also like to fight
Gerbils like to run round a wheel
They find it easy, it's no big deal
They eat seeds
They like to run around in weeds
Gerbils can bite
They sometimes come out in the night
They sometimes escape when you're asleep
They also like to leap
But I know who's got the best gerbil of all
My gerbil of course, Snowflake.

Hazel Thompson (11)
Carolside Primary School, Clarkston

Music

Music's got a beat
In a concert or the street
From jazz to rock
They're all kinds
And some of them even blow your mind
All around the world, music is played
All around the world, singers are paid
Music is great
People love it
It's the best thing
I've ever heard
Music just never stops going
But if it did
It would keep on flowing.

Nathan Zochowski (10)
Carolside Primary School, Clarkston

Percussion

Cymbals crashing
Bass drum booming
Hi-hat clashing
Snare drum rolling

Percussion is my hobby
I've played it for a while
I like to play the drum kit
And I play it with great style

I play it in my house
I play it in my school
My teacher is Miss Dow
And she is very cool!

Ross Gunning (11)
Carolside Primary School, Clarkston

The Broken Window

Ball in hand, me in goal
Long throw out to Mick
Controls and lifts it to his knee
A magician, knows every trick

To the head, then the knee again
And hangs it in the air
On the volley, a power smack
All we could do was stare

Like a missile, off it went
By now, we feared for the worst
Old lady Truman's window smashed to bits
Hope that ball's not burst

I darted in and slammed the door
That day Mick walked alone
For there was music to be faced
And he was facing it on his own

Mick quickly got the ball
Old lady Truman coming to the door
Mick jumped over Mrs Truman's wall
Old lady Truman came, Mick didn't make it in time.

Callum Sweeney (11)
Carolside Primary School, Clarkston

Seasons

Seasons come and seasons go,
Summer sun and winter snow,
Autumn leaves and springtime flowers,
But the seasons are always changing.

In summer there is bright, warming sun,
It's the time of games, happiness and fun,
Holidays seem to last forever,
But the seasons are always changing.

In autumn the leaves turn from green,
To red, to gold - it's an amazing scene,
Boisterous winds blow you over,
But the seasons are always changing.

In winter there's frost, fog and snow,
Icicles form and stalactites grow,
Children play on their sledges for weeks,
But the seasons are always changing.

In springtime, there are flowers,
Young lambs frolic for hours,
Joy is as common as the daisies,
But the seasons are always changing.

Karen Barclay (11)
Carolside Primary School, Clarkston

Seasons

Spring is when the flowers are starting to grow
Spring is when we have chocolate Easter eggs
Spring is when the new baby animals are born
Spring is when the leaves start to form on the trees
Spring is fun, as fun as can be.

Summer is when the sun shines bright
Summer is when we go on holiday
Summer is when we splash in the water
Summer is when we wear our shorts outside
Summer is fun, as fun as can be.

Autumn is when the leaves fall off the trees
Autumn is when the wind starts to speed
Autumn is when we have fun in the leaves
Autumn is when the drains get blocked badly
Autumn is fun, as fun as can be.

Winter is when we make snowmen in the snow
Winter is when we use our wellies most
Winter is when the streets are bare and cold
Winter is when the sun is on holiday
Winter is fun, as fun as can be.

Aimee Kay (11)
Carolside Primary School, Clarkston

The Night

The night smiled upon the Earth
And flicked her silver hair,
'I wonder what it would be like,' she said,
'If I lived down there?'

She moved her gaze to a village
And saw an infant child,
She looked into his dreams
And in them he ran wild!

The night smiled upon the Earth
And smoothed out all her curls,
'I wonder if they appreciate,' she said,
'What I do for this world?'

She moved her gaze to a mountain
And saw a hiker there,
He looked pretty lost,
So some moonlight she would share.

The night smiled upon the Earth
And admired her silver stars,
'I wonder if the aliens,' she said,
'Can see them up in Mars?'

She moved her gaze to the horizon
And saw the day arrive
And now she knew it was time,
To say all her goodbyes!

Freyja Wilson (11)
Carolside Primary School, Clarkston

Olympic Skaters

See the skaters glide on ice
Each wants to win or pay the price
Olympic medal is their aim
To become the champion and get the fame
No matter what, each one is bold
To try to win Olympic gold
Jump, spin, twist, turn
Until their muscles begin to burn
The hours of training they put in
To be the best and try to win
Not all can win at this tough game
You see we're different, not all the same
Time, decisions, judges think
While the skaters wait at the rink
We see the score, the crowd all rise
Now we know who's won the prize.

Kirsten MacGregor (11)
Carolside Primary School, Clarkston

Scary Parties

S cary parties are such fun
C all your friends, they can come
A ll dress up, come and play
R eal good menu for today
Y ou can have . . .

P unch made from blood
A nd lizards' eyes and human beans
R abbit legs stew
T ail of dragon (Cantonese style)
I t's fun, so come
E verything is good, but best of all
S trawberry ice cream and chips.

Ross Brown (11)
Carolside Primary School, Clarkston

The Clock

Continuously ticking,
Never stops ticking,
Keeps on ticking,
Sitting there ticking.

Time passes,
Time goes on,
Children growing,
Children being born.

People growing old and wrinkly,
Some more meaner or more friendly,
Continuously ticking,
Never stops ticking,
Never will stop ticking.

Timothy Dunn (10)
Carolside Primary School, Clarkston

Spring Has Begun

Winter's gone, no dull or grey
Millions of daffodils in sweet array
Buds opening reaching the sky
Their colours so pleasing to the eye
What does this season mean to me?
It means spring has begun.

Days are longer and much brighter
Raincoats and wellies
Puddles and brollies
Children playing in the street
Hopscotch, skipping ropes, what a treat
This is the season, the start of fun
What does it mean?
It means spring has begun.

Rachael Lamarra (11)
Cathedral Primary School, Motherwell

The Giant

In the old castle, not far away,
Near the village with the little bay,
There lives a giant so big and scary,
Last time he visited the village, he stole Mary.

Today he came just as the clock struck two,
With a booming voice that screamed, *'Boo!'*
He laughed as everyone ran to their homes,
He picked up a girl and said, 'I smell tasty bones.'

As he walked to his castle the girl began to cry,
When the giant told her to wave goodbye,
The giant finally approached his home,
He pushed the handle which was a comb.

Inside the castle was a trampoline
And the most beautiful sofa you have ever seen,
He said to the girl, 'I am not really that scary,
If you look over there, you will see Mary.'

'All I wanted was some friends, you see,
As I am so big and scary, nobody wanted me,
Stealing Mary was not very clever,
I just wanted a friend forever and ever.'

'I understand,' said the girl, 'you just wanted a friend,
Mary and I shall be your friends to the end.'

Chloe McAlpine (11)
Cathedral Primary School, Motherwell

The Monster Who Lives Under My Bed

I am positive there is a monster under my bed
My mum won't believe me, she thinks it is all in my head
I told her, it's green, pink and blue
But she says, it mustn't be true
He is big and hairy, but don't be scared
He is just like Shrek, millions of layers
He is big and fat because he loves eating fries
But I have told him he must cut down on the pies
Only thing wrong, he has big, cheesy feet
They are really smelly and don't go down a treat
He is one of my best friends along with Billy and Tilly
Oh, and don't forget all about Millie
He has a massive bed that only I can see
And a toilet so he can have a wee wee
His house is much larger than mine
It is just like a big straight line
I am kind of confused how he fits under my bed
But he says that's his secret that stays only in his head
My monster is always alarmed
I think he is my good luck charm
I take him everywhere I can
I hope we run away together, I have started to make a plan
I love my monster, I wouldn't change him for anything
Not even a necklace or a golden ring
It if got to exchange another monster for mine
I would say no 'cause mine is the best of all time!

Erin Eadie (11)
Cathedral Primary School, Motherwell

Seasons

There are four seasons in the year
And for you, I'll describe them here.

Spring begins with flowers starting to bloom,
Sunnier days end the winter gloom,
Time to get outside and have some fun,
Watch the lambs and calves as they play and run
And then there's Easter with all its treats,
Toy fluffy bunnies, chocolate eggs and lots of sweets.

Summertime is here to stay,
Especially when the sun comes out to play,
Fun days out and holidays abroad,
So much to do, no time to be bored,
No school, no homework and staying up late,
Makes this season really great.

Autumn arrives and flowers fade,
School returns and new friends are made,
Plants' colours change and trees turn brown,
Fallen leaves sweep across the town,
Days shorten as the clocks are set back,
Conkers in the playground go *whack!*

Winter turns everything white
And it is such a beautiful sight,
Making snowmen with the snow,
Sleighing down hills I love to go,
Santa comes and brings us cheer,
Christmas is the best day of the year!

Claire Connelly (11)
Cathedral Primary School, Motherwell

Going To The Pictures

I like going
To the pictures with Dad
He buys so much popcorn
It's totally mad.
And chocolate and sweeties
And hot dogs and nuts
Mum says not to do it
'Cause he'll ruin my guts.

I like films about animals
And films about wizards
I saw one about dinosaurs
The great big lizards.
Some films make me laugh
And some make me cry
But I love them all
I'm not sure why.

I like the huge screens
And the music so loud
And the sound of the laughter
Of the folk in the crowd.
I like going
To the pictures with Dad
And I like telling people
Of the good time I've had.

Rachel McCann (11)
Cathedral Primary School, Motherwell

My Seasons

My summer days are filled with joy
And lots and lots of fun
I spend them playing in the pool
And lying in the sun.

My winter days are freezing
And filled with lots of rain
I spend them wishing spring would come
And bring the sun again.

My spring days are quite happy
And blue skies begin to show
I spend them watching gardens bloom
And flowers beginning to grow.

My autumn days get cold again
And winds begin to blast
I spend them hoping this year
Will be just as good as the last.

Shaun Nicholls (11)
Cathedral Primary School, Motherwell

Lonely

Lonely, lonely, lonely.
Lonely takes place
When no one is there for you.
Lonely appears again
When no one cares that you
Are late home from school
Or have a fight.
Then lonely fades
When you are surrounded
By loving, caring parents
And your most reliable
And caring friends.
So now I am no longer
Lonely, lonely, lonely!

Natalie Thomson (11)
Cathedral Primary School, Motherwell

An Ode To Bubbles - My Goldfish

Like most kids, I have a pet fish
She lives at home, in a glass dish
In the morning I give her food
I get no thanks, she's quite rude.

I called her Bubbles, that's quite neat
She swims with fins, she has no feet
I touch her scales, it feels like slime
Looking after her, takes all my spare time.

In the evening, I'm washed, ready for bed
Always just after Bubbles has been fed
I know she is happy, she smiles at you
Just like me, she is God's creation too.

Then one morning, washed and dried
Downstairs to see Bubbles, I found she had died
It made me so sad, that I wanted to cry
Why, oh why, did she have to die?

That night I buried her, I said a prayer
Telling her that she is now in God's care
I wish she were here
But I know she's always near.

Bobbie Paterson (11)
Cathedral Primary School, Motherwell

Dragons

Dragons are cool, dragons are fun,
Dragons hide from everyone,
Flying around,
So they can't be found,
Listening for any strange sound,
They may seem scary especially at night,
But watch out, it's you that could give them a fright.
Their colour may be red or even green,
Dragons are cool, but don't like to be seen.

Jordan Lewis (11)
Cathedral Primary School, Motherwell

The Enchanted Wood

Deep in the mountains, lies an enchanted wood,
Enchanted creatures searching for food.
Fairies and pixies flying around,
What will we find lying on the ground?

When it is light, the birds make flight,
But when it is night, they are nowhere in sight.
Cosy and warm, all the creatures sleep,
Everything's quiet, you could hear a peep.

When it is morning, all the creatures awake,
At lunch the rabbits bake a beautiful cake.
When it is dinner, everyone eats,
Sitting near the fire, getting the heat.

When night falls they look for a place to rest
And make a warm and safe nest.
The moon shines down, ever so bright,
As all the creatures say goodnight.

Mhairi Duncan (11)
Cathedral Primary School, Motherwell

The Toys

When the children go to bed
To the doll's house the toys are led
Dolly makes them something to eat
Maybe she'll make a special treat!

After that the toys they play
Until the first signs of day
They run and dance about
Careful Teddy - make sure you don't shout!

When the children start to wake up
Robot is there to prevent a slip up
So that when the children walk through the door
The toys aren't moving anymore!

Rebecca Fitzsimmons (11)
Cathedral Primary School, Motherwell

The Colours Of The Rainbow

When a rainy day goes and out comes the sun
It's time to go out to play and have lots of fun
But when you are out, look up in the sky
You'll see a lovely rainbow, way up high.

First there's red, a joy to see at night
Then you know, it's shepherds' delight
Orange is a colour bright and cheery
When you wear it, you're never weary.

Then there's yellow, that always makes me happy
It makes you feel good and not so snappy
Next it's green, the colour of grass
When it's frosty, it's like treading on glass.

Blue is water, so rough yet so calm
But not so good when it runs over the dam
Indigo is a blue so deep
Like the colour of the sky when you're asleep.

Violet, a colour, a name and a flower
Along with pink, admired as girl power
That's all the colours of the rainbow
Up in the sky, a colourful show.

Colette Carr (10)
Cathedral Primary School, Motherwell

I'm Hungry

I'm hungry and there's nothing in the fridge,
Let's go to the supermarket and round it we will whizz!

Look, there's some broccoli, which I call green trees,
Can we get them Mum? Oh please, please, please!

Where are the yoghurts? Are they over here?
There's no more left, oh dear, dear, dear!

Let's go home and then I'll eat,
All the good stuff until I'm eight!

Amy Stark (11)
Cathedral Primary School, Motherwell

The Seasons

Spring wakes up the plants and flowers
We then see lambs and April showers
Daffodils, eggs and the Easter bunny
Hot cross buns and a special day for Mummy.

Summer with long, hot, sunny days
Barbecues, fun and time to play
T-shirts, shorts and paddling pools
And we are not at school.

Autumn days are crisp and clear
And leaves fall from the trees
The clock goes back and days get shorter
We wear scarves and mittens to keep us warmer.

Winter winds blow on your face
Ice on the window makes a pattern of lace
Snowmen, sledging and Santa too
I wonder, will he visit you?

Aimee Flanagan (11)
Cathedral Primary School, Motherwell

The Weather

There is all different weathers from sunny to rain
But it doesn't bring us down in pain.
The wind is weird because it blows and blows,
You don't know how far it's going to go.
Everyone loves snow wherever you go
When you go on holiday you expect some sun,
That's what makes your holiday such fun.

If it's a blizzard then don't expect to see a lizard
If it's cold and you're growing tired and old,
Move to where it's sunny and gold
I love all the weather, sunny or cold.

Stefan Ward (11)
Cathedral Primary School, Motherwell

His Pain Alone

He looked at her bed
Staring with fear
And his eyes filling with tears.
He thought about all the fun times,
Bad times and scary times they had spent over the years
And now she was dying.
He watched the silvery rain pour down the crystal windowpane.
He remembered the first time they set eyes on each other,
He was only a puppy, all alone,
She was a teenager,
Had no time for dogs,
But when she set eyes on him and he saw her,
There was a bond between them.
He now faces the lane of loneliness,
No one knows how he feels,
It's his pain alone.

Shaun Donnelly (11)
Cathedral Primary School, Motherwell

A Visit To The Carnival

My mum took me to the carnival
What an exciting thing to do
I saw lots of spectacular rides
Bright and colourful too.
I went up high like a bird in the sky
I smelled all the delicious food
Lots of marshmallows and chocolate fountains yum, yum, yum!
I went on a twister that went as fast as lightning, *whoosh, whoosh, whoosh!*
When I came out of the carnival
I thought it was fun, fun, fun!

Michael McCabe (11)
Cathedral Primary School, Motherwell

Fairies In The Garden

There are two fairies that live in my garden,
Their names are Lilly and Jill.
Lilly is noticeable from the window sill,
They live in the tree in the middle of my garden,
They both wear pink, silk dresses,
One brighter than the other.
Jill's wings are green,
The lightest green I have ever seen.
Lilly's wings are red
Just like her flower bed.
They dance all night in the moonlight,
When I wake up in the morning
They are snoring instead of yawning.
That's my fairies as you can see,
When I see them flying, I wish it was me.

Sarah Lloyd (11)
Cathedral Primary School, Motherwell

The Toy

Once there was a boy,
Who bought a new toy,
But the toy that he bought,
Was no ordinary toy.
During that night
When the boy was asleep
The toy woke up
And began to creep.
Spreading dreams all over the world
Then the toy rushed back and froze still
When the boy woke up
All he found
Was a lifeless toy
Still on the ground.

Fiona Ross (11)
Cathedral Primary School, Motherwell

Witches And Demons

Where was I? This place seemed strange,
As I looked around, everything had changed.
In the distance I could see,
A tower as tall as could be.

Suddenly, I heard a cackle coming from up high,
Above, a witch on her broom, flew across the sky.
On the back of her broomstick, perched a little cat,
Its coat was as black as the witch's pointy hat.

As I walked alone in the murky night,
Something unusual was coming into sight.
Gremlins, goblins and many more beasts,
Came together for a special midnight feast.

Feeling scared, I started to shake,
I tripped and felt the ground quake.
Waking up I started to scream,
As I realised it all was just a dream.

Nicole Leggate (11)
Cathedral Primary School, Motherwell

One Little Horse

One little horse all alone,
How he survives nobody knows!
During the summer and during the winter,
He waits alone and in his eye a glimmer.
He survives the heat and the cold,
That one little horse so brave and bold!
He waits in the field for his master to come,
But all he sees is the shining sun,
He'll watch the dog with its bone,
That one little horse all alone!

Lauren McShannon (11)
Cathedral Primary School, Motherwell

Gliding On Ice

Everyone thinks that winter is great
But the thing I love most is that I get to ice skate
When I glide across the ice I feel beautiful and strong
When I'm on the ice nothing can go wrong.

Moving along you may trip or fall
You may feel weak and very small
But if you work hard and try again
You'll be back on the ice and won't feel the pain.

Ice skating isn't easy I have to say
But I could practise night and day
I dip and turn like a graceful swan
The excitement starts when I put my skates on!

The crystal-white ice is like a blanket of snow
I never want to be off of it, that's what I know
Living the dream, my spirit runs free
When I'm on ice, I can just be me.

Katie Cunningham (11)
Cathedral Primary School, Motherwell

The Song Of The Elephant

Thumping noises like an earthquake
Bang, bang, bang as the ground shakes
Splash, splash, splash goes your long, showery nose
The water spits out like a non-stopping hose
Swish, swish, swish goes your whippy tail
You have more water in your nose than a whale!

Your ears swing floppily to and fro
Boom, boom, boom everywhere you go
Your eyes are like marbles shining in the dark
Your skin is as hard as a lump of bark.

Lauren Greer (10)
Cawburn Community Primary School, Pumpherston

The Abandoned City

My footsteps echo as I walk the forgotten city's streets,
Homeless children stare in the gloomy silence,
They have given up,
In desperation and hopelessness,
My hometown is now unrecognisable,
Lifeless, roofless, windowless,
Hills of rubble once called homes.

The sadness of the city is in the air,
People scavenge for scraps of food
To take to their burnt-out homes,
The thin wailing of those who are in pain
Drifts through the streets,
The city has given up in despair.

Rebecca Munro (11)
Cleish Primary School, Cleish

The Scarecrow

Poor old scarecrow, lonely and sad,
Standing amongst the yellow oats,
In the shade of an oak tree.
Made of rusty poles
With a turnip for a head
And straw for his hands.
A warm, woolly jumper,
A pair of old trousers and a worn hat,
Torn clothes to keep him warm.
Scaring the thieving birds,
He protects all of the crops.

Edward Wood (8)
Cleish Primary School, Cleish

The Long Ago City

I stand and stare at this crushed and shattered landscape,
The once proud and grand houses, now lie as mountains of bricks
and slate,
The dusty road is a heap of rubble.

Starved, pale faces peer miserably out from behind charred
and scorched windows,
Abandoned children wander listlessly over the wreckage,
Their lifeless faces full of despair.

Warsaw is unrecognisable now,
Its ruined and deserted buildings,
Left to the wind and the rain,
The long ago city . . .
The city of Warsaw.

Joanne Myerscough (11)
Cleish Primary School, Cleish

The Scarecrow

Old, tatty scarecrow, happy as can be,
Dreaming in the golden grain,
Sticks and straw hold him up,
A turnip on top for a head,
Old dungarees, a shaggy, dirty shirt,
A holey hat to keep him warm,
He chases the greedy birds away
From the breezy grain.

Hamish Gillanders (8)
Cleish Primary School, Cleish

The Chimney Sweep

Lonely, young chimney sweep, climbing with elbows,
Clambering up narrow chimneys,
Brushing down the soot,
Cuts and bruises on legs, feet, hands,
Working hard for his money,
Petrified of losing grip of the hot bricks,
Reaches the top, tired and exhausted,
Dreading the climb back down.

Fred Culley (8)
Cleish Primary School, Cleish

Gymnastics

Gymnastics are fun
Gymnastics are cool
I can do them in the pool

Cartwheels are fun
Cartwheels are cool
I can't do them in the pool

I can do a bridge
My friends can too
We crawl under each other

Competitions are fun
Competitions are cool
Because you do lots of gymnastics

I can do the splits
So can you
We can do them together

Handstands are fun
Handstands are cool
We can do them together

Everything here is fun
Everything here is cool
I can do some in the pool.

Emma Findlay (8)
Clerkhill Primary School, Peterhead

My Best Friend

My best friend,
Has brown hair
Also she has blue eyes
But most of the time
She is slow getting changed
So I have to wait and wait
Wait for her!

My best friend is kind
And friendly too
She helps me
So I help her too
She can keep all my secrets
She can make me laugh!

My best friend
Is called Chloe!

Abbey Thornton (8)
Clerkhill Primary School, Peterhead

Creature Comforts

The flatworm
Scales the sea
But it doesn't fly
Around
Like a bumblebee.

The wasp scales
The skies
But it doesn't have
Moonlight eyes.

Bumblebee buzzes
And stings
It's kind of like a
Bring, bring, bring.

Rory Thomson (8)
Clerkhill Primary School, Peterhead

Wrestling

There are different wrestling moves
There's the F5 FU
Backdrop
619 choke slam
Batista bomb
The bear hug too.

There are wrestlers
That jump and punch
They kick
They fight a lot.

There are wrestlers
That are tall
There are wrestlers
That are small
Strong with big muscles.

There are different weapons
For the wrestlers to use
A ladder, steel chair
Trolley sledgehammer
Number plate too.

Ewan Patterson (8)
Clerkhill Primary School, Peterhead

Colour Of Things

The sky is blue
The grass is green
Roses grow bright and red
Yellow and orange is the sun
And brightly shining
The mud is brown
Where the green stems grow.

Oranges are nice
Flowers are pink
Gold is a colour that shines.

Silver is a cold colour
Cream is a hot colour
It does not matter
If it is hot or cold
They are all very nice.

The blackboard is black
The white board is white
Elephants are grey
And that is all for now.

Abbie Turnbull (8)
Clerkhill Primary School, Peterhead

Colours

Blue is like the midnight sky
Red is hot like the hot, hot sun
Green is like me on a boat
Yellow makes me think of the stars
Orange makes me think of a bursting volcano
Gold is like my shiny medals
Pink is the colour of a rose
Silver is the colour of the top of the sea
Colours, colours, beautiful colours.

Shannon Wallace (10)
Colliston Primary School, Colliston

Fireworks

Fireworks fly in the sky
Hit the clouds really loud
They make a really awesome sound
When they hit the ground
I love the way the colours sprout
Out of sight in the night
Then comes the Catherine wheel
Big 'n' round, spinning round
Fireworks, fireworks, I love fireworks!

Ross Thompson (10)
Colliston Primary School, Colliston

Rabbits

R abbits are so beautiful
A nd so cuddly and so cute
B ut I love mine the best of all
B ut they need attention after all
I give him loads of hugs and kisses
T reats they love lots and lots
S o give them carrots, yum, yum, yum.

Carla Ingram (10)
Colliston Primary School, Colliston

Cats

Little cuddly ball of fur
Snuggled up on her big bed
Playing with her small toy
My little cuddly ball of fur.

Lauren Cargill (10)
Colliston Primary School, Colliston

Seasons

Spring, the time of sudden showers
Rain patters on my umbrella
Pitter, patter, pitter, it's stopped
The sun is shining, smiling on the Earth
As the trees sigh gently in the breeze
That is spring to me.

Summer, the time of endless sunshine
Sunflowers grow tall and yellow in the fields
Turning their faces to the warm glow of the sun
As the boats float gently by on the calm, blue sea.

Autumn, the time of wind and blowing leaves
Leaves fly down from trees high above the ground
People scuffing along, wearing wellies, kicking leaves
That is autumn to me.

Winter, the time when snow comes down
The clouds are white at night
And when you wake, Jack Frost bites
Christmas coming, snow-covered trees
That is winter to me.

But whatever the season
Whenever the time
The world always looks simply divine!

April Shepherd (11)
Colliston Primary School, Colliston

A Highland Cow

He is scary and grumpy
He goes mad if you touch his horns
His coat is woolly and golden
He is cool.

Owen Jamieson (11)
Colliston Primary School, Colliston

Sparkie

Sparkie is my rabbit, I love him to bits
I love him when he's bad
And I love him when he sits
He's got a lead and loves to walk
But I really, really, really, wish he could talk.

He's white and ginger with floppy ears
He's mostly happy but sometimes dreary
He loves to eat cabbage and carrots
But I still think he's the best rabbit.

Abbie Louise Anderson (10)
Colliston Primary School, Colliston

Final Lap

It's the final lap
You're at the back
You take a turn
You've taken over
You're almost there
You don't realise
You're the winner!

Christopher Jones (10)
Colliston Primary School, Colliston

Night

Night's terrifying tread through towns and streets,
With a dreary stare from his face.
His ripped, ragged clothes stained with blood,
Moving places without a trace.
His long locks of greasy hair swaying in the breeze,
His slanted red eyes glaring all around,
His scabby, slim mouth rotted and torn,
Night roams the world, but never to be found.

Alia Linnegan (11)
Crail Primary School, Crail

Night

Night is a kind person with deep blue eyes,
A very truthful person, never telling any lies.

She moves steadily and slowly, not making much noise
And everybody loves her like the little girls and boys.

As she runs over the hills, her long, jet-black hair
Follows her, flowing everywhere.

She lives in a cottage way up on the hill
With a little running brook surrounded by daffodils.

Every night she creeps silently into my dreams
She comes by flying, so it seems.

Night is the owner of the big wishing star
Night is the owner of the skies so far.

Night dazzles everybody in her long black dress
No matter what the occasion she never looks a mess.

Miko Blockley (11)
Crail Primary School, Crail

Night

Night is kind and beautiful
Safe and quiet
She gives me sweet dreams
She is like a caring grandma
She has a bright funny face
And her eyes are light blue like diamonds

Her dark brown hair is as smooth as silk
She moves slowly and softly on her way
Home to the clouds
She is my friend
She stops me from getting nightmares
She makes me feel safe and happy.

Ryan Watson (11)
Crail Primary School, Crail

Night Is A Caring Grandpa

Night is a kind man,
He makes me feel comforted,
He makes me feel safe.

Night makes me think of sweet dreams,
He is like a caring grandpa to me,
He is a comfy, warm, safe and cuddly man.

Night has a kind, crinkly face,
His eyes are warm and sparkly,
He has a smiley mouth.

His hair is white like Santa's,
His clothes are like clown clothes,
He moves like a steady man.

Night lives on a star,
He keeps me warm and safe,
He makes me feel safe.

Michael Mayes (11)
Crail Primary School, Crail

Night

Night is cheery and reassuring
She's safe and comforting
She makes my dreams sweet
Night is like a caring best friend
The way she's so gentle and kind
Her eyes are as blue as blue crystals
Her mouth, when she smiles
Is like the shape of the moon
Her hair is as smooth as silk
She moves quickly and smoothly
Along her way home
Her house is a cottage
But inside it's like a palace
She plays with me
And makes me feel safe and happy.

Terri McGillivray (11)
Crail Primary School, Crail

Night

Night is unknown,
Scary but innocent,
His scared face is covered by a shadowy hood,
His dried, pale lips utter strange words,
As he glides over the land,
Casting eternal darkness wherever he goes.

Night is lonely,
Not one friend,
He never talks
And moves so swiftly
That nobody knows him.

If you ever meet Night,
You won't remember it,
As you will fall into a deep sleep
And be cursed with nightmares for the rest of your life.

Night will stay in his dark, damp castle,
Thinking terrible thoughts,
When 8pm comes he will leave his home
And cast darkness all over the Earth.

Jack Mills (10)
Crail Primary School, Crail

Night

He walks alone in the dark,
No one can hear the beat of his heart,
His silver hair, with streaks of gold,
Only he knows what the future holds.

His soft face and eyes like stars,
That sparkle and shine like a caring grandpa's,
He moves slowly through the quiet streets,
No one knows the people he meets,
He is a comforting person and makes you feel warm,
He makes you feel safe when scary dreams form.

Emily Grieve (11)
Crail Primary School, Crail

Night

Night is a foul tempting demon,
He will fill your mind and soul with dark thoughts,
His hooded gaze would terrify some,
His white bony hands will pull you down.

Night is swathed in black robes
And from within his cowl, he stares outwards,
His unblinking gaze can see all,
Behind him a trail of black smoke.

Night glides over the ground,
He stands between waking and sleep,
He will guide you to rest,
He will put you to sleep.

Night lives in infinite darkness,
Until the sun sinks below the horizon,
When he conjures up dreams and nightmares
And sends the masses to bed.

Thomas Smout (11)
Crail Primary School, Crail

Night Is An Evil Demon!

Night sends a shiver up my spine,
When he comes creeping through the shadows;
He is unsociable
And should not be trusted.

Night makes me have nightmares,
About him capturing and hurting children;
Just imagining his deep red eyes,
Makes me feel vulnerable.

Night has greasy, messy and unwashed hair
And a mouth full of razor-sharp teeth;
He wears torn and muddy clothes
And moves as silently as a grave.

Kane Lennie (11)
Crail Primary School, Crail

Anger

Get anger away . . .
Put it in a cube and shut the lid
Think of blue, calmly look at it
Kick a ball as hard as you can
Grasp a handful of snow till it melts through your fingers.

I play with my dog - take him for a walk
I kick the ball with my foot
He brings it back with his nose
I laugh
Back home we go
I have juice, he has water.

I squeeze a softball - it helps me calm down
I feel like hitting a drum, thinking it is my anger
I think I am on a Moto X gripping the handlebars as hard as I can
Rev . . . rev . . . rev . . . it calms me down
I'm calm now!

Dale Stirling (10)
Crail Primary School, Crail

Night

Night is a thief - a killer
He is horrible, nasty and bitter
He lives in an unlit alleyway
Where he creeps about the bushes
He has a devil tattoo on his neck
And he gives you nightmares
Just thinking about him
He has a low, husky voice
And carries a cold, sharp, steel knife
You'd better watch out or he will
Steal your things . . .
Jump out at you . . .
And kill you!

Dawn Woodcock (11)
Crail Primary School, Crail

Night Is A Lovely Lady

Night is a lovely lady,
Kind and comforting,
She makes me feel safe,
Her eyes like twinkling stars
And her mouth a half-moon smile.

With hair like flowing clouds
And her cloak long, dark and warm,
She moves in orbit,
Slowly circling the Earth,
Sighing softly like a gentle breeze
And at the setting of the sun
She comes - in control,
Sweeping steadily,
From her mysterious mansion,
Beyond the horizon.

Carla Mead & Sean Beattie (11)
Crail Primary School, Crail

Night

Night is evil
Night is a vampire
It makes you feel worried
Its face is wrinkled, like crumpled paper
Shiny sapphires are his eyes
With scruffy hair and dry lips
He moves by hovering
With his velvety black cloak
His hissing voice
Puts a shiver down your spine
He lives somewhere on Mount Everest
In a cave with bats and spiders by his side
If he gets in your house, watch out
He'll give you
Nightmares!

Scott Patterson (11)
Crail Primary School, Crail

Anger

My anger is like a gorilla beating its chest
My anger
My anger is the sound of thunder and lightning
On a bad day
My anger
My anger is like two Indian bells clashing together
My anger
My anger is the colour of red and black
My anger
My anger is like a motorbike revving up
My anger
My anger is like nails scraping down a blackboard
My anger
My anger is like hot, hot fire
My anger
My anger is like drums being hit hard
My anger
My anger is two people wrestling
My anger!

Lisa Mowbray (10)
Crail Primary School, Crail

Anger Is . . .

Like a lion roaring
A darkish blue
A circle 'cause it can't get out
Stormy Saturn
Bongo drums
Stupid
A chewy sweet
A roaring bear
Street fighting
An aeroplane taking off
Lightning.

Sean Barnes (10)
Crail Primary School, Crail

Anger

Everything is black
I feel like there's an elephant behind my back
It's thunder and lightning
I'm not frightened
There's no going back out
I'm trapped!

I am playing tennis, hitting the ball
It's flaming hot so I drop it on the spot
The toxic waste taste makes me sick
A rock band singing, mad; makes me go crazy
My hands are burning in the box
The guitarist is so good doing rock
I wish I was on the top of the world
I went on a motorbike going so fast
Now my anger has gone, I'm just going to rest at last
And that's my anger!

Nicola Mayes (10)
Crail Primary School, Crail

Anger

Always steaming up deep red,
Never turning blue again,
Gritting my teeth day and night,
Ending, not till tea tonight,
Raging round with a groan.

Going non-stop, raging round,
Not going to stop,
Great power in my rage,
Entering . . .
The octopus in my head,
Trying to shoot it dead,
Raining on my head,
Slipping the anger out of my head.

Anthony Mitchell (10)
Crail Primary School, Crail

Anger

Anger, anger, calm, calm, down!
Grumpy black monkey prancing around
Grumpy black monkey, big, large and round
Anger, anger, calm, calm down!
Grumpy black monkey a big large storm is coming
Grumpy black monkey playing football when a storm is coming
Anger, anger, calm, calm down!
Grumpy black monkey tastes sour, it's rather nasty
Grumpy black monkey his sound is rather noisy
Anger, anger, calm, calm down!
Grumpy black monkey slapping roughly on the bongo drums
Grumpy black monkey swinging through the air, fast, just like
                                                    a motorbike
Grumpy black monkey has finally calmed down
Grumpy black monkey calmed down with a pillow in his hand
Anger, anger, calm, calm down!
Grumpy black monkey is not angry anymore
Grumpy black monkey is finally adored
Anger, anger, calm, calm down!
Grumpy black monkey is not making a sound
Grumpy black monkey is peaceful once more
Anger, anger, calm, calm down!

Ruth Dickson (10)
Crail Primary School, Crail

Angry Then Happy

When I am angry, I feel . . .
Like a mad dragon spurting red flames,
A boulder thundering down a mountain,
The rough sea pounding on the rocks on a thundery night,
A drum thundering like a rocket rumbling,
A mouthful of spicy curry, just swallowed, going red inside
And then . . .
My puppy sits beside me, cheers me up, cuddles me,
I am happy again.

Megan Reilly (9)
Crail Primary School, Crail

My Temper

When my temper gets out of hand,
I feel like a rock and roll band.
When my temper is really bad,
Guess who shouts at me . . . my dad.
When my temper is locked away,
I feel I'm on a swing where I soar and sway.
When my temper makes me scream in a pillow,
After that I feel as soft as a willow.
When I'm out of my strop,
I just have to say to myself to
Stop!

Hazel Forgan (9)
Crail Primary School, Crail

Anger

There's a wolf in me . . .
A bad wolf
With red blood from his teeth
And fire in his eyes
When my wolf is angry
He's standing on the sun.

Lauren Brown (9)
Crail Primary School, Crail

Anger

Red as blood
Roaring lion
Raging storm
Rectangle
Running, running
Red tomato
Roaring sounds
Rough.

David Morales Miller (10)
Crail Primary School, Crail

Anger

When I'm angry I feel flaming red and pitch-black
When I'm angry I feel like a rhino wanting to charge
When I'm angry I feel like lightning going to strike
When I'm angry I feel like a very pointy star
When I'm angry I feel like I'm the ground where a marathon takes place
When I'm angry I taste like a bad, sour apple
When I'm angry I sound like a lion's *roar!*
When I'm angry I feel like I've slipped on seaweed on the rocks at the beach
When I'm angry I feel like a drum beating like thunder
When I'm angry I feel like the sea crashing against the cliff walls
When I'm angry I feel like a rocket blasting off . . .
Five . . . four . . . three . . . two . . . one!
And then it's gone.

Laura Wilson (10)
Crail Primary School, Crail

Anger

My anger is like fire
It can start up at any time
I'm like a man-eating lion
That can taste like very hot curry
When I get angry I go all red
I scream into my pillow
The sound is like a clashing cymbal
All I want to do is punch a punch bag
All I think about is a very loud blow from a saxophone
That penetrates my ears
I can hear a motorbike thundering past
The forecast is for thunder and lightning
If I had a rocket
I'd make it a triangle
Then I'd *zoom* off into space
Towards the midday sun.

Claire Thomson (10)
Crail Primary School, Crail

Anger

All I see is red and black
I feel like a wolf with a bloody cut
The weather around me, no sun
Lightning is all that is there
I feel like a triangle is cutting my head
The only sport I seem to play is hurling
Being hit with sticks
I taste vomit in my mouth
An air raid siren killing my ears
I feel like a thousand pins are stabbing my heart
Anger kills me.

Peter Rhodes (10)
Crail Primary School, Crail

Nimbolo

I'm Nimbolo, the slayer, ha, ha, ho, ho,
A strange ol' name ye may say,
So I'll tell ye how I won my title.
Long ago, on a fine summer's day,
I was the son of a mighty king,
Me and two hundred others,
Half of them were sisters, of course
But the other half were brothers.
We were all out on a picnic one evening,
In a forest all dark and thick,
Suddenly we were under attack,
By ten thousand vermin, 'twas bad.
Some began shouting for help,
An' others for Mum and Dad.

Scott Bramley (9)
Crathes Primary School, Crathes

Football Team

My brothers make a really good football team,
They're never mean,
They're always so keen,
I think they should be seen,
To see how good they are,
They always take the car to the course,
There are different ways of playing football, you know,
If there is a course, they always want to go,
As I told you, they're ever so keen
And that's why I think they should be seen in the football team.

Nicole Galloway (9)
Crathes Primary School, Crathes

The Thin Boy

Once there was a boy
Who was terribly thin,
He would not eat a thing his mother gave him.
He really was quite dim
So here is his story, right from the start.
When he was young he ate well
But when he was six he would not eat a thing
So day after day
He grew thinner and thinner
Then one day he died.

Hamish Leeson (8)
Crathes Primary School, Crathes

School

School is the best
But is a lot of stress.
The work is fun
When it is done.
Lunch is yum
But can hurt my tum.
When it is time to go
I am glad my work is done.

Rhayzl Park (8)
Crathes Primary School, Crathes